Selling Our Death Masks:

Cash-For-Gold in the Age of Austerity

Selling Our Death Masks:

Cash-For-Gold in the Age of Austerity

Yesenia Barragan

Winchester, UK
Washington, USA

First published by Zero Books, 2014
Zero Books is an imprint of John Hunt Publishing Ltd., Laurel House, Station Approach,
Alresford, Hants, SO24 9JH, UK
office1@jhpbooks.net
www.johnhuntpublishing.com
www.zero-books.net

For distributor details and how to order please visit the 'Ordering' section on our website.

Text copyright: Yesenia Barragan 2014

ISBN: 978 1 78279 270 3

A CIP catalogue record for this book is available from the British Library.

Design: Stuart Davies

Printed and bound by CPI Group (UK) Ltd, Croydon, CR0 4YY

We operate a distinctive and ethical publishing philosophy in all
areas of our business, from our global network of authors to
production and worldwide distribution.

CONTENTS

For the ancestors I never met.

Acknowledgments

I heard the first rumblings of this tiny book sitting in the warm living room of Temma Kaplan's apartment in New York City in the spring of 2012, during a conversation about the enthralling and uncertain landscape of protest and desolation left behind by the Occupy and global Squares moment. Sometime that evening, Temma casually mentioned the striking sight of mountains of cash-for-gold shops that exploded across Spain with the onslaught of the economic crisis in 2008. Pushed along the trail by my own fascination with gold, as both commodity and shiny object itself, I began the project there, hoping to make some sense of the golden mountains and the strange moment we find ourselves in. Cheers to Temma for her support, but most importantly for setting me off without even knowing it.

In writing and thinking about this book, I am especially indebted to *el profe* Michael Taussig (*o sea* Mateo Mina), who I've had the immense privilege of studying with at Columbia University while writing a dissertation on slavery and abolition on the Pacific Coast of Colombia. In many ways, the indomitable spirit of his writing has inspired this book. My deepest love to Mick not only for the foreword, but for re-kindling the poet-historian in me, for pushing me to embrace self-doubt, and for teaching me how to care for the Angel of History.

This book wouldn't have been possible without the help of many, many people throughout Spain, Greece, and Colombia. In Madrid, heart of the cash-for-gold empire, I am grateful to the *compro oro* workers I spoke to at Puerta del Sol, who were kind enough to speak to this otherwise awkward academic and give me a small insight into their everyday worlds and lives. I also must thank Eliana, Tzissous, Malamas, and others at Alpha Kappa in Athens and Thessaloniki for their help with this project and for teaching me about the anti-fascist and anti-mining struggles in Greece today. In Colombia, I am indebted to my *amiga del alma* Rudy Amanda Hurtado Garcés from Timbiquí for her beloved friendship and support throughout the years. In Quibdó, Adaluz Estrada and Alberto Sinisterra Muñoz were dear friends who kindly introduced me to the city and Chocó, and I am also grateful to Francia Elena Marquez from La Toma for teaching me so much about the AfroColombian struggle. And my deepest gratitude to Zero for publishing the piece.

I am also indebted to my *gran familia*, blood related or otherwise, that I've accumulated over the years. My sisters Gina Rodríguez-Drix and Natalia Buier gave me crucial feedback on this piece, as did my dear friend Michael McLean, and I am grateful for their time and advice. My deepest love goes to the Rodríguez-Drix family (Gina, Julian and Xiomi), Chris Spannos and Harpreet Kaur Paul-Spannos, Alison Keenan, Paul Buhle, and Viviane Saleh-Hanna for their constant support throughout writing this book. I am especially grateful to my sister Dara Bayer for blessing this project with her amazing artwork, and for reawakening the spirits among our sister circle. *Ashé*. Finally, to my beautiful sisters, Vanessa, Gigi, and Karina for their feedback and unrelenting love and support, for giving me strength and helping me become the woman I am today; to Karen, Joe, and Emily for their love and care over the years, for embracing me as a daughter and sister. And to Mark, the love of my life, without you this book, and everything else, would be unimaginable. ("It was a moment like this, do you remember?")

Foreword: The Curse of Gold

Michael Taussig
January 30, 2014

It is not easy to deal with a curse as old as mankind, to keep it at arms' length and, if possible, transform its ominous power into healing. Yet this is what Yesenia Barragan achieves—to the extent possible—in her fast-paced brilliant, and exceedingly original history of gold and its roller coastering life under contemporary capitalism. In an enviably short book, this deft writer has created a living history of the present that maintains a cliff-hanging tension connecting through gold, the pawn shops of Greece and the foreclosed homes of Detroit with African slave women in the gold mines of the Chocó in northwest Colombia. This is truly the practice of what Walter Benjamin meant by a "constellation" in which the past surfaces unexpectedly as an image in the current struggle not just for survival but for justice in today's terrifying world in which modern slavery vies with that of the past thanks to naked exposure to the so-called free market in which the majority of humankind has been reduced to thinghood, *desechables*, as they say in Colombia, meaning "throw aways" or disposable.

There are profound lessons for us in this pithy work. The first is that yes! it is possible for a very young scholar still working on her doctoral thesis at Columbia University in New York to perceive and to create for us an eye-opening history of the world—and to do so while immersed, so to speak, in the humid archives of a town sunk in the Colombian jungle. The town is Quibdó, capital of Chocó province in northwest Colombia, subject to the highest rainfall in the world as well as the burden of what used to be accessible gold gravel in its many rivers. It was that gold that led to African slavery starting in the eighteenth century and whoever visits Quibdó today cannot but feel this legacy in the stark decrepitude of its mildewed buildings, the silent vastness of the Atrato river with its massive dugout canoes, and the solitude of its gaunt cathedral on the river bank, rising as an unfinished monument to an unconquerable nature. What a contrast to the glittering gold that poured out of this sub-aqeuous world for close to three centuries, making Colombia the main gold producer of the Spanish empire. With the sky rocketing price of gold today, another form of violence saturates the region; guerrilla, mafias, and paramilitaries demanding their share.

The author is as much an ethnographic fieldworker of the pawn shops of present day Europe, especially Spain and Greece, as she is an assiduous historian culling state and church archives in Quibdó, Popayán and Bogotá. Two histories and two sets of stories collide. In Europe, gold reasserts itself amongst the poor and the ravaged middle classes today as a charmed substance saturated with personal feeling as well as with mystic valor. With shame and despair people hand over wedding rings and family heirlooms to the "cash-for-gold" stores that have sprung up like mushrooms. For many centuries gold has been squirreled away for just such a day that, however, nobody really thought would happen. Most of the time if people had any savings it went into the bank! Oh my! Didn't they always say the bank was the safe place. Forget that shoebox under the bed. The bank was where money was safe? Every one of us had their chance to be their own little capitalist. Oh my! Gold was for old-fashioned paranoid people who liked a gold tooth in their mouth or a flashy ring. Then what happened? The banks proved the mystic hollowness of what is called "the economy," far more mystical than millennia of myth making concerning gold. The other history connecting with this, of course, is that of the slaves producing the gold that went into that tooth and into that flashy ring and into that wedding ring that now goes to the "cash-for-gold" stores springing up like mushrooms. Yet these stores too will soon disappear, as if obeying some frightful Law of Nature as all the rings and teeth are pawned and there is no pathetic "sentimental gold" replete with family history left. Moving back and forth the author spans centuries and continents bound by the charm of gold.

What I also find remarkable is the author's ability to write simply and clearly for everyone. There is an ethics and politics in this fact alone. We could call it "low tech intellection," quite unlike that of most academics and historians. In other words she shows how you can be both in this world as well as writing and talking about it from afar, you can be immanent as well as transcendent, territorializing as well as de-territorializing as you work on your geopolitics.

What is more, the author instructs us in the ways of doing justice to both the local and the global. She re-winds the local history of a far away place like the Chocó with world history and with the current desperation in Greece, Spain, and the USA following the world financial collapse of 2008. This is a "method"—to use a rather abrasive term—that makes me re-think what "globalization" means and how we might address the fractious and complex ways that the local interacts with the global wreckage that is history and do so without sacrificing the local specificity which, in the final analysis, is what reality is all about—real people living real lives made epic by the play of capital—i.e. gold.

This, however, is not the only cause for wonder that this little book arouses. What is also at stake in this "history in the present" is a specifically mystical encounter with history itself. All storytelling and hence all telling of history has its quotient of mystery and entangled connections with lost time and the place of the emotions and the body in memory, even if professional historians spend a great deal of exuding denial of this and pride themselves, in this regard, on their lack of poetry and blunted sensitivity to the spirit that moves history, rarely more so than with respect to gold, that stupendously empowered symbol of beauty, value, greed, and strife, making it, ultimately, the curse of mankind—at least in humanity's modern incarnation. Not that it was all that different in ancient worlds, except there the sanctity of gold was formalized in ritual and recognized for its connection with death, menstrual blood, and the sun, as with the Kogi Indians of the Sierra Nevada de Santa Marta in Colombia, not that far from the Chocó, who buried gold in the form of sacred figurines along with the dead.

Yet how strange it is, how monstrous and pathetic it is, that the famous Gold Museum in Bogotá, physically and institutionally in the heart of the *Banco De La República*, has nothing to say about African slavery, given that it was that slavery that made the colony so rich and that along with the silver of Potosí kick started what Karl Marx called "the primitive accumulation" necessary for the take-off of modern capitalism. What the museum does is celebrate—and fetishize—gold in relation to ancient, pre-colonial, Indians. In other words both the bank and gold find their ideological prowess in the White Man's fantastic imagery and bizarre affect concerning ancient America—as with the alleged "shamanic origins" of Colombian goldwork lavishly displayed by the Gold Museum with its New Age archaeology along with haunting flute music.

It is this same affect which undergirds the legends, myths, and glitterance of gold, while the Black people of the Chocó and elsewhere are rendered invisible by history's airbrush. And that is the point of the fetish, is it not, at least in Marx, that labor is absorbed into the object—in this case, gold—such that while people drop out of sight, things such as gold and capital are seen as self-empowered, hence gold's strange vitality, let alone its curse. So there are different histories and different historians for them. There are those who blindly succumb to the fetish, and those who embrace it so as to use its powers to transform the curse—the curse of gold.

This is the sparkling achievement of Yesenia Barragan.

"Without gold nothing is possible, people are dead even while living."
— *Brahmapurāṇa*

The Beginning, or An Origin Story

"Perhaps truth is a woman who has reasons for not letting us see her reasons? Perhaps her name is—to speak Greek—*Baubo*? Oh, those Greeks! They knew how to live. What is required for that is to stop courageously at the surface, the fold, the skin, to adore appearance, to believe in forms, tones, words, in the whole Olympus of appearance. Those Greeks were superficial—*out of profundity*."
—Friedrich Nietzsche, *The Gay Science*

"Since when the custom of inserting mirrors, instead of canvases, into the expensive carved frames of old paintings?"
—Walter Benjamin, *The Arcades Project*

In the beginning, before there was light, there was the sun.

Dark, it was completely dark at first. As the sun pulled herself up out of the darkness and ascended to the black, lonely heavens, she left behind a magical yellow trail of sweat that dripped slowly down from the celestial skies onto the moist sand and rocks below. Over hours and decades and centuries, the sun's holy sweat gathered together and hardened into the deep pockets, recesses, and rivers of the earth, searching for hiding places to bury pieces of herself. And so, GOLD, the holy sweat of the sun was born.

Soon, though, the big secret was out. People everywhere began to seek the sun's divine sweat, and soon enough they started to shape beautiful amulets and masks to ward off the darkness from whence she came. Later, temples were erected in reverence to her. Of course, it wasn't heaven, but it was nowhere near the second wave of darkness coming ahead.

The second darkness came and enveloped the skies. Men on horses with long, weird beards and more horses. They named it the Conquest. Maybe this is where our story should begin?

Soon, the golden temples were melted down and the sun's sweat was hardened yet again by human hands and shaped into round coins and fancy chairs, traveling the world in scary boats, exchanged for black and brown bodies in chains and heaps of salt and spice.

Or should we begin here, on the boat and in the company of death and the divine sweat?

Hours, decades, and centuries later, after sitting still in golden clocks and necklaces and coins, long after the brutal voyages, collecting dust in the old basements of banks and jewelry boxes, the people rediscovered the protective properties of the holy sweat, as they inched closer and closer and closer to the third darkness.

The third darkness came and enveloped the skies. Men in cars with hard-pressed suits and more cars. They named it the Crisis. Armed with briefcases and calculators, they began to crack open the earth and little by little there was less and less foundation that more and more people began to slip into the darkness of the earth.

Terrified, everyone knew what was coming. And so those remaining ran to the banks, and rummaged through the closets and underneath their mattresses in search of the sun's holy sweat that they knew had to be given away. There was no other way out.

Some gathered together privately in suburban housewife living rooms, where they threw Gold Parties. The rest of them, the massive lot of them, they streamed into the countless, new cash-for-gold shops that the Crisis had erected, where they stood in line for countless hours to trade in the holy sweat for a few minutes to breathe before they too might slip into the cracks of the earth. "In Gold We Trust," read a sign outside of this new temple. Soon, the golden clocks and necklaces and coins were melted down yet again by human hands and made their way into the pockets and bank accounts of the gods of the third darkness.

But now, stripped of the sun's protective holy sweat, how could the people possibly ward off the darkness from whence she came?

* * *

This book began with a simple question: why did the number of cash-for-gold shops skyrocket following the economic crisis of 2008, that is, during the Age of Austerity?

In 2010, at the height of the crisis, cash-for-gold shops tripled to nearly 500 in the southern region of Andalucia, Spain, one of the areas hit the hardest by the economic policies of austerity in the country. Only Madrid rivaled Andalucia with more than 700 shops in 2011, while Madrid's Luxury Westin Palace Hotel became the site of Europe's first ever gold-vending machine. In Greece, the European capital of the Regime of Austerity, 90% of 224 officially registered cash-for-gold shops opened in 2010. Across the United Kingdom, "pop-up" cash-for-gold stands increasingly dot urban and suburban shopping centers, amidst rumors of swanky "gold parties" in the living rooms of struggling English housewives. "Business is very good, you can really feel the crisis," claimed Alexia Messi, a cash-for-gold shopkeeper in Rome, who owned seven cash-for-gold shops as of 2012.

Why bother with cash-for-gold shops? Well, as Daniel Miller argues in *Stuff*, things and objects, including the cash-for-gold shop itself, are important "not because they are evident and physically constrain or enable, but quite the opposite. It is often precisely because we do not see them. The less we are aware of them, the more powerfully they can determine our expectations..."[1] Objects are powerful because they "work by being invisible and unremarked upon, a state they usually achieve by being familiar and taken for granted."[2]

This book therefore urges us to not only *see* and breathe life into the elusive cash-for-gold shop, but furthermore, taking the Italian shopkeeper Alexia Messi's claim seriously, it seeks to *really feel* the crisis from inside the shop. And like Walter Benjamin, who asked why, at that particular historical moment, mirrors were being inserted into "expensive carved frames of old paintings" instead of canvases, it attempts to examine why these shops suddenly exploded after 2008 and what it all means for us.

For now, however, we'll begin at the end.

Chapter 1

Compro oro, dinero ya!
Cash-for-gold in Spain

Perhaps there is no better time of year than Christmas to bear witness to it. And there's no better place in the world than Madrid's infamous *Puerta del Sol*—where hordes of visitors spill in and out of her flashy shops, *comprando sus regalitos*, faster, slower, then faster. Spanish for Gate of the Sun, Madrid's *Puerta del Sol* was the center of the radial network of Spain's historic roads, the economic lifeline of the early modern Spanish kingdom.

But far from those days of eternal glory when gold from her distant colonies was pumped into her hungry veins, today's crisis-hit Spaniards are increasingly visiting Sol's thriving *compro oro* (cash-for-gold) shops to give *back* their gold, in exchange for hard cash. There are no official figures, but *El Diario de Sevilla* reported that in Seville alone, there were more than 200 cash-for-gold shops in 2012, far beyond the mere 8 that scattered the city's landscape in 2008.[3] Only Madrid rivaled Seville with more than 700 shops in 2011.[4] Dressed in flashy neon yellow gear, the *compro*

Los Compro Oro **Guys. Photo by Mark Bray.**

oro guys, the industry's walking salesmen—the vast majority of them Afro and *mestizo* immigrant men from Latin America—beckon your business, becoming a fixture of a struggling Spain in the age of austerity.

When asked about her weekend shopping at *Puerta del Sol*, a French woman I met gasped in bewilderment, "I even saw the COMPRO ORO guys on horses!" "Two of them," she specified. Mouths agape, the surrounding crowd of listeners were equally shocked.

The *compro oro* guys on horses. Imagine that! What a sight to behold! And all in the King's glorious plaza, the great-great-great-great grandchildren of her colonies, sitting upright on her horses. But this time, the rules of the game have changed and the stakes are higher than ever.

* * *

"Life changes when you lose everything," recounted Manoli Cortés, an older Spanish woman, one afternoon.[5]

At 65 years old, Manoli had seen it all. She had lived through Franco, the Spanish dictator who ruled the country from 1939, after Spain's bloody civil war, until his long anticipated funeral in 1975. Franco lingered at death's door for seemingly endless weeks before giving in. Manoli may have joined the thousands of listeners crowded around the national radio or television to hear the final announcement of Franco's death, along with his farewell message to 'his people' which he had written just weeks before.

"Spaniards," the anchor read on behalf of Franco's ghost, "When the hour comes for me to surrender my life before the Most High and appear before His implacable judgment, I pray that God may receive me graciously in His presence, for I sought always to live and die as a Catholic." The souls of thousands of disappeared fighters howled from unmarked mass graves across the Spanish countryside. The representative of the recently departed Franco continued: "Do not forget that the enemies of Spain and of Christian civilization are alert. Keep watch yourselves and subordinate every personal concern to the supreme interests of the Fatherland of the Spanish people..."[6]

Thirty-eight years later, in 2013, Manoli was sitting in a new room, a "typical Spanish living room: immaculately clean, filled with family photographs and dark wood furniture,"[7] far away from that crackling radio or television set.

But, truth be told, Manoli was not sitting in a typical room and these were not typical times. Nope, not even close. As of January 1, 2013, Spain's unemployment rate reached an unprecedented 26%, while President Mariano Rajoy of the right wing, pro-austerity *Partido Popular* (also known as the *PP*, or jokingly, as the *Partido Peligroso*, the Dangerous Party, by activists) continued to raise taxes, lower wages, and make unparalleled cuts to education, healthcare, pensions, and social services.[8] Meanwhile, a report discovered that 22% of Spanish households were living in poverty as of 2012, and nearly 600,000 homes weren't generating any income. The prognosis for the following months, or even years, does not look any better.[9] Joined by so many other Spanish families who had lost just about everything in the wake of this very unnatural disaster, Manoli moved what remained of her belongings into an empty building, forming the *Corrala Utopía*—a growing network of occupied buildings in Seville with coordination from the 15M movement (sometimes referred to as the *indignados*). Outside the building, a spray-painted banner declared: "*Ni gente sin casa, ni casas sin gente*" ("Neither people without homes, nor homes without people.")

Around the corner from Manoli's very atypical apartment, you'll find Ana Lopez, one of *Corrala Utopía*'s oldest residents at 67 years old, along with her 71-year old husband Pancho, a former flamenco dancer. In the last few years, she tells us, Pancho suffered three heart attacks, in addition to health complications related to his diabetes and asthma. After falling behind in their mortgage payments (in 2010, it is estimated that Spanish banks foreclosed on more than 100,000 homes, while an estimated 130,000 homes remain empty in the Seville region alone), the elderly couple was evicted. They slept for several weeks in the lobby of their former building before settling into *Utopía*.

"I have grandchildren," Ana added, "When I die I would like to be able to say to myself that they will have jobs, homes and a happy life."[10]

"The *corralas* are important," she reminds us, "...They show that we can help ourselves and each other. I don't know what the future will hold for any of us, but one way or another I believe that this will be a successful fight. I have to, otherwise I wouldn't be able to sleep at night."[11]

Before *Utopía*, 44-year old Toñi Rodriguez was forced to spend the night in her car while her "son was living with my mother. Every morning I use to get up at 6am to take him to school. I thought I was going to lose him to the social services. I needed to find a place for us to live. It was either live in the street or do something else."[12] And get this—even if you are evicted from your home, you are still legally obligated to pay the remaining mountain of debt on your evicted home! Can you imagine that? Sleeping in your car, or in the lobby of your former building, being forced to write out checks for something that is no longer even yours.

And yet, while more and more Spaniards are erecting their cardboard homes in the street corners of Madrid or Málaga, or taking over lonely buildings gathering dust, others have taken another road with no return. The week of February 11, 2013 was a slice of time destined to remain a dark moment in Spanish history, for in that week alone four Spaniards took their own lives before the police and bank officials could evict them from their homes.

It all began on February 12, when 56-year old Iñaki Vesga, a resident of the sleepy town of Basauri in the Basque region, committed suicide before the police arrived.[13] It was reported that he left a note to his family saying *"no podía más"* ("I couldn't anymore").[14] Miles away on the island of Mallorca, on that same day, an elderly couple, aged 68 and 69, overdosed on their prescription medicine while awaiting eviction. Their son found their bodies.[15] A few days later, on February 14, a 46-year old man hanged himself in Alicante, a beach town on the eastern coast. A driver by profession, he was unable to pay rent for the past few years. According to neighbors, he had warned people of his impending actions.[16]

Unfortunately, that haunting week of February 11, 2013 came as no shock. Months earlier, in November of 2012, 53-year old Amaya Egaña, a former municipal councilwoman for the Socialist Party, took her life by jumping off her sixth-floor balcony. Apparently, a legal team from the local court with foreclosure papers rang her doorbell and knocked on her door several times before a locksmith was ordered to open it. When they opened the door, they discovered her standing on a chair on her balcony, ready to commit the act.[17] It has been reported that since the beginning of 2012, over 100 Spaniards have taken their lives over their financial despair.[18]

And then there are the 'survivors,' those who managed to push on, even for just a few days, after being evicted. But even they are not safe from austerity's grip. In March, an unnamed 56-year old man hanged himself in Alicante, ten days after having been evicted from an apartment he was renting. He had been unemployed, unable to find a job for quite some time.[19] In the wake of these events, thousands of Spaniards demonstrated across the country against deadly mortgage policies. Off in the distance, a growing crowd of housing activists and supporters in Madrid shout, *"No son suicidios, son asesinatos!"* ("They're not suicides, they're murders!")

But once the crowds disperse and night casts its shade onto

Aftermath of an anti-foreclosure action in Madrid.
Photo by Mark Bray.

the capital's winding streets, another crowd begins to form. First, there are only two or three people. Fifteen minutes later, there are nearly ten. Instead of monuments or statues, meeting points for mass actions around the city, the crowds gather around the garbage bins of closed supermarkets, searching for a night's (or even a week's) meal. Victor Victorio, a 67-year old Peruvian immigrant, was among a crowd one evening. In 2008, he lost his job in construction, and searched for whatever he could lay his hands on. This time, it was peppers, tomatoes and carrots. "This is my pension."[20] The situation has gotten so bad that the city of Girona "resorted to installing locks on supermarket trash bins as a public health precaution."[21] But which public health matter are we talking about here?

Well, at the very least the darkness of the night can veil the scavenging crowd's faces from the damning looks of judgmental neighbors. What do they know anyway? For some, it beats the painful embarrassment of showing up in soup kitchens. It is said that some families escape to food pantries in distant towns so as to avoid seeing their friends or family members.[22] The crisis is a deep embarrassment for us all.

* * *

"So, do you know anyone who's been to a *compro oro* shop before?"

"*Pues,* it's like going to the psychologist, or better yet the soup kitchen," said Veronica, a Spanish teacher I met in her early forties, "You don't tell people that you need to go, because you're ashamed, so we never know who among us has been."

It could be anyone. It could even be Veronica, but we'll never know. She shrugged.

Like Veronica's elusive response, you can't escape the *compro oro* shops no matter where you go, where you turn. As of July 26, 2012, there were nearly 15,000 shops in Spain.[23] It all went haywire when the price of gold, responding to rattled investors seeking some kind of payback-stability, jumped dramatically in the wake of the economic crisis (i.e., in 2009 gold spiked from 723 Euros to 921 Euros, a 27% increase!).[24] Once King Gold, reliable monarch that he is, manifested the might of his rule the shops began to mushroom.

In the northern province of Galicia alone, there were more than 100 shops in 2011. A Galician shopkeeper from a *compro oro* store named *Oro Efectivo* commented that he had seen "numerous wedding and engagement rings" passing through his shop, leftover remnants of broken-up marriages and engagements, victims of the crisis.[25] (That being said, according to the Spanish Judicial Council, the divorce rate in Spain was 17% lower in 2011 than in 2006. "There is no doubt that the crisis is pushing people to stay together," reported José María Redondo, a spokesman for the council. Still, despite the delay in divorce, separated couples are finding novel ways to cohabitate while weathering the economic storm. According to Álvaro Cavia, a divorce lawyer in Barcelona, some couples are zoning off spaces in their cramped apartments with tape on the floors![26])

(Could it be, I wonder, that the wedding rings handed to the Galician shopkeeper came from the feuding Mr. and Mrs. Esteban and Maria Fuentes Ruíz? Did they also tape down their apartments like their counterparts in Barcelona, or did they find new ways to negotiate their new lives? And where were the kids or the dog allowed to roam?)

In 2009, there were 27 shops in Castile and Leon, birthplace of Queen *Isabel I de Castilla*, who famously backed Christopher Columbus's mad plans westwards in search of a quick route to the East Indies. By 2010, there were 76 in the region.[27] And heading south from Castile and Leon to Seville, where Queen Isabella received Columbus in her royal court, the 8 cash-for-gold shops in 2008 expanded to more than 200 by the end of 2012, with nearly 400 in the greater Seville province. It is said that competition between *compro oro* vendors in this area is so intense that shopkeepers rent out empty stores and often *leave them empty* just to keep competition away.[28]

And then there's Madrid and our beloved *Puerta del Sol*, the heart of the *Compro Oro* Empire. Here, at the Gate of the Sun, there were up to 200 shops as of 2012, the largest concentration

of shops in the entire country. The greater Madrid area boasted 700 shops in 2011; the highest anywhere in Spain and a giant leap from the 200 in 2007. "I came here to sell some pieces of gold," said Rosa, a Spanish woman who sold some of her stuff at a shop in *Puerta del Sol*, "some pieces of gold, a necklace, a ring and a medal. You need to rip yourself apart from them because soon the payments will come, and you'll want to get rid of them before they rob you. I'm going to pay the water, the gas, the electricity, food, that's what I'm going to do." Another unnamed Spanish woman also added, "It's a shame for me to have to sell my gold, the jewelry I had, and little by little, I have nothing left... Today I have nothing."[29]

("Life changes when you lose everything."[30])

"You can't eat gold," said María José Rigo, a cleaning lady and recent widow from the island of Mallorca, the same site of the suicide by the elderly couple that dark February week. In late 2010 and early 2011, María José had already sold three bracelets and four rings, but that wasn't enough to make ends meet, especially after her husband passed away and the debts started to mount. Waking us up from this fetishistic love affair with this shiny yellow stuff, María Jose indeed reminded us, or maybe even warned us, that you can't eat gold. (But can gold eat us?)

Whatever the case may be, you can't talk about cash-for-gold shops in Spain without also talking about its wealthy cousin: the gold vending machine.

You heard me right—a gold vending machine. In fact, Madrid's very own Westin Palace Hotel is home to Europe's first-ever "gold-to-go" machine, which debuted in 2010.[31] Bring in any extra Euros you have lying around the house (I believe 40 Euros is the lowest you can submit), and you'll get a shiny gold bar in return. The first such machine was set up in the lobby of the Emirates Palace in Abu Dhabi earlier that year in 2010. In 2011, a company announced it would install more than 2,000 Gold ATMs across China within two years.[32]

"Yeah, that's for *los ricos*," the rich people, commented a young, pretty blonde cash-for-gold salesperson I spoke to off *Puerta del Sol*. "The rest of us," she added, touching the edges of her stylish fingernails, "they come here, to the *compro oro* shops." And for those who can't make it to the exclusive Westin Palace, you can buy bars of gold elsewhere, from shops like *Oro Directo*, where Spain's middle and upper classes exchange their Euros for stability in the shape of a yellow bar.

The irony isn't lost on anyone, not even the *compro oro* guys. "Some people sell their jewelry, a ring or whatever, get the money, and then buy back the gold they sold!" exclaimed Alejandro, an older Ecuadorian cash-for-gold vendor I met in late December when I asked him about the mysterious Gold ATMs. He shook his head. "It's crazy."

* * *

No matter whom you ask, everyone seems to have made up their mind about them, the *compro oro* guys. One journalist cautioned readers against seeing them as "architects [of the crisis]." Rather, he warns, they are "the paid-by-commission stewards of the recession."[33] Another journalist, in the same spirit, said that the *compro oro* guys are in fact the "thermometers of the crisis," constantly taking the collective temperature of the bed-ridden world economy. The less you see them, so it is said, the better the financial prognosis. *Good riddance boys!*

But in addition to their multifaceted job description as stewards and human thermometers, they've also been called "soldiers of gold,"[34] for the hours they spend in their commanding, fluorescent yellow *compro oro* armor drifting back and forth in front of their shops. Or perhaps this journalist also saw them on horseback and mistook them for the ghostly great-great-great-great grandchildren of the long dead *Rey*-something-the-third. Or maybe all of us have it all wrong.

"What can I say," said José, a *compro oro* guy I spoke to one chilly late December afternoon just a few steps away from *Puerta del Sol*, "I'm just trying to make ends meet."

José one of the *compro oro* guys I spoke with, is from Mérida, Venezuela, a city tucked between the breathtaking Venezuelan Andes. Back in 1558, Spanish conquistador Juan Rodríguez Suárez named the settlement after his hometown of Mérida in Extremadura. Venturing to the "New World" in search of gold years after the fall of the Aztec and Incan Empires (1521 and 1532, respectively), it is said that before founding Mérida, Suárez "ran up against opposition in the Valley of the Mocotíes from Indians whose style of attack earned them their nickname of dancers or *bailadores*." But, like so many other *conquistadores*, Suárez pushed his luck, for he was charged with "mistreating Indians and exceeding orders by founding a settlement," and was eventually arrested.[35] Although the majority of indigenous people living in the area were violently displaced from their homes and forced to settle in the 15 new towns established by the Spanish after the conquest, many of them fled to Mérida in "search for better economic opportunities."[36] Soon, they would find themselves working alongside enslaved Africans in the region's grueling cacao plantations.

When I asked José for his thoughts about the crisis, he couldn't help but laugh, playfully slapping my shoulder. *"Hombre, en Latinoamérica, siempre hemos tenido 'la crisis.'"* ("Man, in Latin America we've *always* had 'the crisis.'")

Yes—I wanted to nudge him in that cold-silly-social-scientist kind of way—but *when* did this seemingly infinite crisis begin, José? When *exactly*? Can you give me a specific day, month, and year please? (According to Marxist economist Christian Marazzi, the shift from Fordism to post-Fordism occurred exactly on October 6, 1979,[37] so such calculations aren't totally out of the question). Can you offer me anything, José?

No?

Okay, fine, just a year will do for now. So then, José, what year did it all go wrong? 2008? Or maybe 1982, when the Mexican debt crisis set off Latin America's rapid economic decline, eventually paving the way for the neoliberal regime of the 1990s?

Or is it that you want me to push back farther, deeper? (Will you be able to pull me up from out of here, from the cracks of the earth?)

Is it 1558?

"I've been here about six years now," he says, quickly pulling me up out of the hole, "Of course people are still selling their gold with Christmas and all, to buy some toys for the kids, but about two or three years ago, there were more people selling, going to *compro oro* shops ... it's not like that anymore, it's like everyone has sold most of their gold already." Yes, it is true, there is only so much gold to go around, being the finite shiny physical substance that it is. There's bound to be an endpoint. But, José adds, "we still get tourists coming in from around the world, from England, the United States, or Germany, they come in sometimes just to see how much their watch is *really* worth."

A fun little social experiment.

We're running out of time, and things to share (quite frankly), so in between his occasional shouts of *Oro! Oro!*, José offers his last words, "What else can I tell you, about my time out here." He laughs. "It's just damn cold!" But, who knows, he says, why don't you talk to my co-worker, pointing to a tall, black man with a New York Yankees cap a few feet away from us. After thanking him, I walk over.

"*¿Hola, cómo estás?*" I start off, before going off into my typical slightly-awkward-yet-friendly introduction of my project on the crisis and cash-for-gold. He's an older man, perhaps in his late forties, and soon I discover from his accent that he's from DR, the Dominican Republic. At first, he seemed to have welcomed me openly with a friendly smile, but immediately after I gave him the lowdown of my curiosity, his face turned stone cold. "We can't talk to you about these things, not in front of the shop, about our customers, I don't know why José told you those things." He looked off angrily towards José, who was busy passing out leaflets to passing shoppers, huffs of warm air emptying from his mouth out into the cold winter breeze.

I tried to explain that I was only interested in his experience working for the shop, nothing confidential, but I soon realized that I had lost him. And now I'm worried that I may have jeopardized José's job. Shit. A few seconds later, a young Spanish couple (or perhaps siblings, it was unclear) approach him, say a few things to him in a very low voice, and he immediately escorts them to the shop upstairs and doesn't look back.

Apparently, this reaction is not entirely unusual. In fact, I didn't expect to be able to speak with many *compro oro* workers, for the vast majority of articles I read claimed that most of them refuse to speak to journalists (or the nosy writer-academic that I am). Reasons range from potential issues of customer privacy to concerns about feeding into the poor publicity surrounding the *compro oro* business. You see, *compro oro* shops, the newest addition to the pawnshop family, are often seen as parasitic (a topic I'll go into a bit more in the following chapter), as they make their biggest profits from dire economic crisis.

Anyway, I had better luck a few days later. That afternoon, I met Alejandro, the same gentleman I mentioned briefly before, an older man who was wearing a black baseball cap and thick blue sweatshirt under his *compro oro* vest while standing in a plaza just off *Puerta del Sol*. "You're Ecuadorian, aren't you?" he said to me almost immediately, with a sly smile. "I could tell from your face, the roundness of your mouth." My mouth? We quickly bonded after he discovered that my father was from the port city of Guayaquil, his hometown.

He traveled that long distance between Guayaquil and Madrid nearly 10 years ago, in 2002 to be exact, before the infamous Madrid train bombings in 2004. "It was easier to come before that," he said, "the bombings changed everything." His wife, also Ecuadorian, came before him, in the late 1990s and was working "taking care of old people." But more than the bombings, he added, the economic crisis really shifted the destinies of so many Ecuadorians living in Spain. "All the *ecuatorianos* I know are either leaving to go back home to Ecuador, to France, or the United States. It's gotten so bad here."

Indeed, it is true that so many Ecuadorians are leaving, going elsewhere and especially back home where, at the very least, as Alejandro noted, "we have some family members to look after us, even if they're terrible." In fact, the country's President, Rafael Correa, a quasi-socialist and sometimes-enemy-sometimes-friend of the United States government (see the Julian Assange scandal), created a program in 2008 called *Plan Bienvenid@s a Casa* (Welcome Home Plan) to try to lure the Ecuadorian diaspora back home by offering, among other things, loans start a business or financial resources to build a new home.

It really wasn't until the 1990s that Spain began to see such a large influx of immigrants, especially from Ecuador and elsewhere in Latin America. "I remember going to high-school in the early-to-mid 1990s," a Spanish friend told me one afternoon, "Everyone, every single student was Spanish. Now, it's different. You can't go to school in any city without being in class with Ecuadorians, Dominicans, Colombians, Algerians..." (What will it mean then, I can't help but ask, to be 'Spanish' years from now?) Before the 1990s, Ecuadorians used to head north to the United States, like my father who joined his parents in Hackensack, New Jersey in the early 1970s in search for the long awaited dream life which never really came.

But then, between 1994 and 2004, Ecuador got into big trouble. During that era, the country saw more than eight presidents, unemployment spiraled, and more than 16 banks closed between 1999 and 2000. Slowly, and then quickly, Ecuadorians started to trickle out beyond their borders.[38] After increasingly stringent American immigration policies clamped down on migration in the late 1990s (and tightened, of course, after September 11th), the US was no longer seen as the go-to destination. Spain, on the other hand, didn't require visas for Ecuadorians (that is, until 2003). Moreover, an undocumented trip to the US could cost up to $12,000, whereas the Spanish legal alternative fell between $3,500 and $4,000.[39] By September of 2009, there were approximately 550,000 Ecuadorians living in the United States, whereas 700,000 were living in Spain.[40] This all stopped, as Alejandro mentioned, in 2008 with the emergence of the crisis.

"A few years ago," he said towards the tail end of our conversation, "I used to make 2,000 sometimes up to 3,000 Euros a month in the construction business." After the housing crash in 2008, those jobs are no longer an option. "So I'm stuck here with my wife and our two children. *A ver que pasa* (Let's see what's going to happen)." 2,000-3,000 Euros a month. That's quite different from the 1,000 Euros that many *compro oro* guys get paid during 'good months.' Temporary workers, they work on contracts that can last as long as three months.[41]

Before parting ways, Alejandro shared some of the little English that he knew—"the beautiful lady"—with a bit of a wink. Yeah, I got the message. While pulling out his business card, he also made me promise to find him a book that would help him learn English "quick." "You know, English can help me leave, I gotta get back home."

 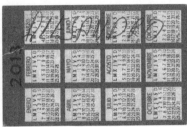

But unlike Alejandro, one of the last *compro oro* guys I spoke to the following day, who didn't offer his name but nevertheless spoke to me for a bit, seemed to be trying to stay away, far, far away from home. A tall, black man with a very visible long scar on his forehead, he was wearing a thin jacket—even though it was still pretty cold—under his *compro oro* uniform. I couldn't catch his eyes hiding behind his flashy, dark sunglasses. And although he didn't want to talk to me for very long, he did offer little bits of himself.

"Yes, it's true what people say that *la gente* come up to me crying, saying they don't want to sell their necklaces or rings, all kinds of people, rich and poor…" He looked off in the opposite direction.

"Your accent, you're from Colombia, yeah?" I asked.

For a moment I had his attention. "*Sí, sí,* I'm from Cali," he said, a major city in southwestern Colombia known for its world-famous *salsa* and beautiful women. There was an inexplicable longing in his voice. "Oh, hey," I responded, "My mom's from Pereira," another city just north of Cali, and in the heart of the country's famous coffee district. "And I'm a historian too, I'm writing about the abolition of slavery in *el Chocó* on the Pacific Coast, I spent some time in Chocó, in Quibdó, Istmina, Tadó, Andagoya..."

There was a brief moment of recognition. The names of familiar towns seemed to have awakened something between us. "Well, actually," he paused looking at me, this time straight in the eye. "I'm really from Buenaventura," a major port city on the southern Pacific coast of Colombia, "...well, a fishing village just outside of Buenaventura..." He looked off beyond me.

And just like that, just for a moment, we were both suddenly standing together, in silence, looking out from a small window in a waterfront shack on the outskirts of Buenaventura, looking out towards the expansive, dark blue Pacific Ocean. It's hot, but the occasional breeze from the ocean cools us off temporarily. Gunshots are set off in the distance—turf wars between the drug lord's paramilitaries and members of Manuel Cepeda Vargas Urban Front, a cell of the FARC (Revolutionary Armed Forces of Colombia, the famous guerrilla group) in Buenaventura's slums. In 2007, around the same time, give or take, that he left Colombia, the *New York Times* called Buenaventura "the deadliest urban center in Colombia's long internal war."[42]

And then we're back again, standing in *Puerta del Sol* where we both shiver a bit in the cold, thousands of miles away from that quiet room on the coast.

"That's a long ways away, I can only imagine, no?"

"*Pues,*" he sighs, "*es muy complica'o, muy complica'o...*"

And he's right. It is all very complicated. Very complicated.

* * *

Things didn't get any less complicated for Spain. Just a month before my conversations with the *compro oro* guys, it was announced in November 2012 that the Commission for Environmental Affairs approved a contract for the Canadian-based Astur Gold company to open up a gold mine in the northern Spanish province of Asturias. Nearly 1,680,000 ounces of gold are said to be lodged in the underground mines of the Salave Gold Project.[43] This despite the fact that locals have protested against the mine, proclaiming that it will cause irreparable ecological devastation.[44]

Yet, *Astur Gold* doesn't just promise jobs, it promises *greatness...big-picture greatness...Historical greatness!* for the famed Romans once operated these Asturian mines. "Since Roman times," *Astur Gold* declares on the front page of their website, "gold has been mined in the Iberian Peninsula." Behind the flashing words, streaming photos of ancient Roman chariots. You can almost hear the heavy breathing of the horses, ready for battle.

"As the Roman Empire faded away," it continues, "gold mining was largely abandoned... until now."

Chapter 2

A Very Short History of the Pawnshop

Around the same time the Roman Empire was gradually crumbling in the mid-to-late 400s AD, the world's first ever pawnshop, the ancestor of today's cash-for-gold shop, opened its doors in China, thousands of leagues away from an increasingly ghostly Rome.[45] So much for *Astur Gold's* destiny. Many trace the pawnshop's date of origin to somewhere between 479-502 AD, during the reign of the Southern Ch'i dynasty. It was only later, after 1000 AD or so, that the pawnshop would emerge from across the Ural Mountains into what would become Western Europe.

Thousands of years before one could even begin to fathom the formerly straight-laced History Channel's racy-titled *Pawn Stars* or truTV's even more titilating *Hardcore Pawn*, the first pawnshops in China operated as sacred, primarily charity businesses restricted to Buddhist monasteries, which controlled them for hundreds of years. Later, the enterprise would spread out from the monasteries into the dusty streets of Shanghai and Xi'an, to be operated by everyday businessmen. *But fear not*, the new pawnshop generation must have reminded their predecessors, *you will not be forgotten*, for the new pawnshop vendors dressed in flowing, black gowns in reverence to the commanding, black robes of the past, pioneering Buddhist monks.[46]

Why the Buddhist monastery? One scholar argues that the Chinese pawnshop was a classic historical product of the interaction between a Buddhism relatively new to China and an "advanced" monetary economy. There, in the Buddhist temples, monks accepted and administered funds called "long life cash" across all classes of society: from the estates of the rich deceased to the dirt poor who donated what they could, whether chestnuts or grain, in exchange for prayers to their passed loved ones and ancestors.[47] Behind the closed doors of the temple pawnshop, these mounds of material objects would accumulate over time, producing a steady surplus of capital and paving the way for a transformation in money-lending practices as we know them. The road from the Buddhist pawnshop to *Pawn Stars* is not so distant after all...

But more than that, the first Chinese pawnshop lends extraordinary insight into the high stakes of the game. As T.S. Whelan writes in *The Pawnshop in China*, pawnbroking may have origins in the ancient practice of exchanging political hostages (*chiao-chih*), often members of the aristocracy, from rival states. The character *chih*, meaning "hostage," came to mean "an earnest" or "a pledge," and over time became a generic term for the Buddhist practice of pawning. *Chih-k-u* later referred to the temple pawnshop, while *chih-chü* meant "pawn loans."[48] Pawning literally signified having your objects taken hostage.

This is a stick-up!

But, really, is this so far from the anonymous Spanish woman who we left behind in *Puerta del Sol*, who pawned and eventually sold her daughter's golden communion necklace like so many other anonymous Spanish women, who "little by little," had "nothing left... Today I have nothing."

And what if I can't distinguish between the object and me?

Or maybe, better yet, the gut-wrenching feeling I had, like so many working-class and middle-class Americans, when my parents told me that the bank was demanding *xyz* amount of money or face immediate foreclosure, later, we would discover, because of robot-computer error on their end. It still didn't make a damn difference anyhow. The money was late, and that's how the cookie crumbles. "We wish you the best." I scribbled in my diary sometime thereafter: "I was a witness, a victim, of a stick-up. If they didn't supply $13,532.67 dollars by next Tuesday by 5:30 PM (EST), they'd be out on the streets. Another empty house in Hackensack, New Jersey."

Yet, T.S. Whelan cautions us, while pawning often did not produce ideal circumstances, it was nevertheless "innovative in part because it no longer subjected a borrower to [other forms of] bondage [i.e., forced servitude or permanent enslavement] in the case of nonpayment, but only caused him to forfeit the chattel in pawn, though this might be a vital one such as a padded winter jacket or plough."[49] But what then is a farmer to do without his plough?

* * *

Sometime during the medieval period, pawnbroking made its way from a Chinese peasant's desperate exchanges in Xi'an, across the Urals into the feuding kingdoms of what was slowly becoming Europe. According to British historian Kenneth Hudson, the finances supplied by budding pawnbrokers were sought to quench "the needs of powerful and ambitious rulers, who required money to finance wars and the building of castles, palaces, and churches, and to maintain a standard of living which they considered appropriate to their rank, power, and social position."[50] In England, for example, William the Conqueror encouraged Jews to settle in his kingdom around 1090, where they served as his main pawnbrokers until 1290, when Edward I expelled them at the height of intense anti-Semitism and the Pope's condemnation of usury practices. The infamous Lombards of modern day Italy replaced the Jewish pawnbrokers, but they too were eventually kicked out in 1530, leaving the pawnbroking business to native British merchants.[51]

Perhaps more than any other merchant class, the Lombards left an indelible mark on the history of pawnshops and pawnbroking by forging the international symbol of pawnbroking: three golden spheres suspended from a bar. The exact origins and meanings of the infamous golden spheres are still contested, but scholars know that it was indeed a symbol that many Italian pawnbroking merchants in the province of Lombardy hung in front of their houses. Some say that the balls represent the story of Saint Nicolas, who gave a penniless man three golden balls (or bags, the story changes according to the teller), one for each of his poor daughters' dowries, so that they wouldn't be forced into prostitution in order to survive. Other scholars have pointed out that the symbol may have originated from a medieval coat of arms, such as that of the Flemish van der Beurse family, which had three golden purses representing the bill and commission brokering profession.[52] Whatever the case may be, the Lombard ghosts have lingered in places like Russia, where a pawnshop is called a *dom Lombard*, meaning Lombard house, and Belgium, where they're referred to as *Lombards*.[53]

Taking a cue from the Buddhist monasteries, Italian priests began to establish charitable, religious pawnshops beginning in the mid-fifteenth century, before Isabella sent Columbus off in search of spices, slaves, and gold. In 1440, a priest in Perugia, located in modern day central Italy, founded the first pawnshop, which soon became known as *monte di pietà*, meaning "banks that take pity," providing small loans, mainly in the form of tools such as ploughs, animals, and other implements to needy peasants. Soon thereafter, this model of charitable lending spread across the Alps into France in 1577, into the Netherlands sometime in the sixteenth century, into Spain in 1705 (and her colonies throughout the eighteenth century), into Sweden in 1772, and across Russia during this period.[54]

Yet throughout the centuries, the pawnbroker, being the moneymaker that he is, especially in times of crisis, was constantly targeted as being the progenitor of all shades of social and economic wickedness. Back in England, in 1603, for example, Parliament announced "An Act Againste Brokers," warning that the "counterfeit brokers and pawne-takers, upon usurie or otherwise, for readie money, are growen of late to many hundreds within the citie of London." These pawnbrokers, they declared, "embolden all kinde of lewde and bad persons to rob and steale," and furthermore "no sale, exchange, pawne, or mortgage of any jewells, plate, apparell, household stuffe, or other goods of what kinde, nature, or qualitie the same shall be of ... to any broker or brokers, or pawne-takers."[55] The English painter William Hogarth captured this animosity in his famous series of engravings entitled *The Four Stages of Cruelty*, first published in 1751. In it, he presents two visions of London under the influence of different alcohol: "Beer Street" and "Gin Lane." In "Beer Street," working-class Londoners are busy at work and play, but soon the rotten effects of gin take over the crowd, and the once jostling yet quaint street is transformed into "Gin Lane," where death hangs over falling buildings, babies, and drunken women. As chaos descended and devoured London's underclass, the pawnshop thrived.[56] In the United States during the Industrial Revolution of the nineteenth century, this hate-affair would take on an anti-Semitic air, as the majority of pawnbrokers at the time were Jews who were barred from many other professions enjoyed by the small clique of elite white, Anglo-American merchants.[57] Layers and layers of wickedness.

* * *

The pawnshop would undergo yet another extraordinary transformation in the twentieth century. Hundreds of years after the Buddhist monasteries opened their doors in China, Mao Zedong and the Chinese Communist Party shut the doors of the pawnshop, if only temporarily, while the Chinese Revolution was underway. In the 1950s, after implementing the policy of collectivization and after the People's Bank of China established Citizens' Petty Loan Offices, the Party shut down any and all pawnshops on the mainland. In 1956, the People's Republic officially banned pawnbroking businesses, denouncing them as a "symbol of an exploitative economy."[58] They would only reemerge in the late 1970s once Deng Xiaoping released the floodgates of the market economy.[59] Of course, the Lombard Houses of the Soviet Union faced a similar fate. Under the New Economic Policy introduced by Lenin in 1921, private Lombard houses were banned, before being renamed "household services for the population" in the 1970s and 80s. The number of pawnshops also exploded after Gorbachev's policy of *glasnost* just before the fall of the Soviet Union.[60]

While Mao and Lenin banished the pawnshop in China and the Soviet Union, in Britain a rapidly expanding and powerful welfare state instigated the pawnshop's decline by responding to the needs of working-class Brits (if only momentarily and imperfectly). But this all changed very quickly in the 1980s when Margaret Thatcher's privatization joined Xiaoping and Gorbachev in a neo-liberal remapping of the global financial terrain. Look no further than major British shopping strips in Chatham in Kent or Walthamstow in east London, where instant payday loan shops and cash-for-gold shops now litter the city's streets.[61]

And like the UK, the story in the US is familiar. During the 1980s, the Reagan Revolution's attack on wages and healthcare spawned a tremendous growth in the number of pawnshops as more and more Americans were unable to access conventional bank loans.[62] Decades later this damage remains, for in 2012 alone there were more than 30 million American pawnshop customers per year,[63] and as the long age of austerity reigns down upon us experts foresee more of the same.

* * *

So where does this leave the cash-for-gold shop, the dashing, dandelion-haired cousin of the straight-laced pawnshop? Unfortunately, I didn't find any references to the origins of the cash-for-gold shop, our main character in this play, but through conversations with people across different countries, it appears that she made her appearance at least in an organized fashion sometime in the early 1990s, which seems to make sense since that's when the neoliberal era really got going. From what's been rumored in the United States, she first showed her face on late-night television infomercials, accompanied by an elderly woman who looked just like your grandmother or neighbor in a pink sweater and reading glasses, reclining on a green couch, confessing to us how shocked she was to discover that her "gold jewelry was worth so much!" Can you believe it? God, me neither. Just send it to the number listed below and you'll get fast cash. Money back guaranteed.

And then somehow she managed to escape from the television set, wandering out into the deserted streets, where she started to set up shop near the corner store. My Argentine friend Marina, whose family weathered the storms of the Argentine economic crisis in the early 2000s, caught the first glimpse of her once the banks shut down access to their customers. "They were everywhere then," she told me.

If pawnbroking emerged in the United States with the formation of the modern capitalist economy, where does this leave the cash-for-gold shop? Does it, like the nineteenth-century pawnshop, signal "the relative maturity of capitalism,"[64] or a bizarrely fleeting hiccup, or an irreversible spiral of decay?

Or something in between?

Chapter 3

The Golden Yesenia

"When all the steel has rusted and rotted, and for ever after that, your great cube of gold will still look like new. That is the kind of longevity we all dream of."
—Peter L. Bernstein, *The Power of Gold: A History of an Obsession*

I remember it so vividly now—it was a Barragan family tradition. "*Cuando* you graduate from *su escuela*," my mother told my fifth-grade self in her broken English/Spanish, "*vamos a comprarle una cadena de oro con su nombre.*" ("We're going to buy you a gold necklace with your name on it.") And she wouldn't dare lie. Sitting on the hot, concrete steps of our house, my mother planted the necklace into my tiny palm, its baby diamonds slightly blinding my eyes. There she was, staring back at me: the golden YESENIA, my trusted necklace-companion who I was to proudly showcase around the dreary, working-class streets of Hackensack, New Jersey.

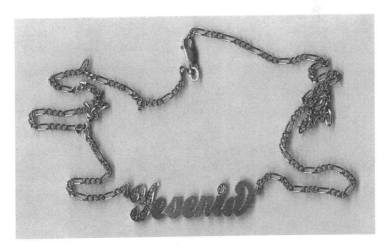

"*Felicidades,*" my mother finally said, sealing the gift with a kiss.

What was it about the golden YESENIA, I continue to ask, that was so important to my mother, to my parents? What did they know that I didn't?

* * *

Longevity. "That gold suffered no deterioration with time and its color resembled the color of the sun may have encouraged the belief that gold was a sacred substance."[65] Maybe even a god itself? So perfect, like God or many gods, so precious and timeless.

How funny, then, the relationship between gold as ETERNAL, as sacred, and the association—across time—of gold with all kinds of secretion, whether shit, sweat, menstrual blood, and even cum. Oh, especially cum. What on earth could be more temporary, more taboo, than that whirlpool of darkish brown fluid?

But yes, in the beginning, it was there, there all along. The sweet, soiled union of gold and all her 'grotesque' companions, what the famed folklorist Alan Dundes called the "gold-feces equation."[66] In Nahuatal, the language of the Aztecs and still spoken today by over a million indigenous Nahua Mexicans whose ancestors survived the Conquest, the word for gold is *teocuitlatl,* a compound of *teotl,* meaning 'god,' and *cuitlatl* meaning 'excrement.' Thus, gold literally was the 'excrement of the gods,' or 'divine excrement.'[67] Holy shit.

In particular, gold was the excrement of *Tonatiuh,* or the sun in Nahua, whose gold shimmerings were the traces of the bodily wastes he released at night on his way to the underworld. According to the Franciscan missionary priest and evangelist Bernardino de Sahagún, who infamously oversaw the making of the Florentine Codex documenting the cosmology of the Aztecs before the Conquest, his indigenous informants described that "'sometimes, in some places, there appears in the dawn something like a little bit of diarrhea,' which is 'very yellow, very wonderful'; it is called the sun's excrement because it is 'good, fine, [and] precious.'"[68]

The French writer Charles Perrault told a similar story. In his fairytale *Peau d'Âne* ("Donkeyskin"), composed in 1695, Perrault tells the story of a mighty king, his beautiful wife, and their beautiful daughter who lived far, far away in a beautiful castle, alongside a precious donkey named Ned who amazingly pooped gold: "Nature had made the beast so pure / That what he dropped was not manure / But sovereigns and gold crowns instead / (Imprinted with the royal head) / Which every morning Master Ned / Left for collection on his bed."[69] Soon, however, darkness struck the royal residence when the queen suddenly died, and the king, at his late wife's urging to find the most suitable spouse, asked for his daughter's hand. Horrified, the daughter sought the immediate advice of her fairy godmother who advised her to demand seemingly impossible tasks from her father in exchange for her hand, including several dresses in the color of the sky, the moon, the golden sun, and finally the hide of none other than Master Ned.

But not even Ned's precious golden deposits could save him from the king's thirst for his daughter, for the donkey was quickly slaughtered. "They bring the skin to her: she's filled with dread / And bitterly bewails the fate that lies ahead..."[70] Ned, nevertheless, comes to the rescue at the end, as the beautiful princess used his nasty hide to smuggle herself out of the castle and into camouflaged safety: "The donkey-skin's a fine disguise, / For nobody could ever guess, / Seeing you in so foul a dress, / That such a filthy thing could hide / Someone so beautiful inside."[71]

The Incas called gold the sweat of the sun, and silver the sweat of the moon. In fact, the holy union of the sweaty golden Sun, Inti, and the sweaty silver Moon gave birth to the Incan empire. According to one creation myth from the Peruvian coast, Vichama, the second son of Inti, asked his father to populate the world after seeing that there was no one present to worship him. Soon, Inti delivered three eggs to earth, one gold, the other silver, and the last copper. The first golden egg, of course, would hatch into the *curacas* and nobles, the silver into women, and the copper into the commoners and their many families.[72]

And according to Mamo Luca, a Kogi priest from the Colombian Sierra Nevada de Santa Marta mountains, gold is "valuable because it is the menstrual blood of Mother Earth in which is concentrated all her power and that can only be extracted through appropriate ritual ensuring that all is harmony at the site of extraction—e.g., 'that the river is good, the animals are good, the plants and the woods are good.'"[73]

Or on the Lembata Island in the Indonesian archipelago, the Kedang people use the word *weren*, or gold in Kedang, to describe liquids including semen. For the Kedang, "gold is like a fluid which emerges from things, it crosses the boundaries of bodies..."[74] The ancient Hindu deity Agni, otherwise known as the fire god, produced sacred semen made out of gold.

In the *Brahma Purana*, the great lord Sambhu said that Agni's golden semen should "be the foundation of all prosperity; he praised gold as a means of purification for the three worlds, as an immortal substance in this world and as dear to the gods, as granting pleasures as well as liberation, as a sacrificial gift ... Without gold nothing is possible, people are dead even while living."[75] The literary critic Marc Shell has also pointed out how, for example, the early fourteenth-century French text *Ovid Moralized* stressed the idea that gold was the substance of God's semen, which entered Mary via her ear, and that Christ was therefore an *aurigena*, or born out of gold, or the many, many medieval paintings of God's inviting golden 'showers.'[76]

"The world delights in opposites," writes Michael Taussig in *My Cocaine Museum*, "Yet this marriage of money and fecal matter

... threatens opposition itself. The two sides of the coin implode, and we are left with exorbitant residue that shoots beyond form. Such is gold."[77]

* * *

It was an incredibly difficult time. "I remember that he gave me this [golden] cross almost as an afterthought," my friend Michael McLean, a high-school literature teacher, artist, and activist from northern New Jersey, told me one afternoon. "He had to take off all his jewelry before he was going into surgery." As Michael's father lay on the stretcher with his hair tucked into a light bluish medical cap, he began to remove his dentures and do all the other "dehumanizing things as you become this object of a medical mission." That's when he gave it to his son Michael, the golden cross, almost as an afterthought. "'Hold on to this,'" his father told him, "'Whatever happens, don't get rid of it.'"

Fortunately, Michael's father survived the surgery. When he told him that he still had his cross months later, his father said that he wanted him to hold onto it anyway. Michael surmises that his father inherited it, the light-weight, golden Celtic cross, from his mother or rather aunt who raised him, but he's not sure. "To me," he said, rubbing the cross with the tips of his fingers, "it's an heirloom," not a religious emblem which it had been for the past wearers, "representing the faith of family, mainly because my father gave this to me just before he went to have liver transplant surgery and it was a moment in which he and I and many of our family members thought he was going to die..." But then, it gets tricky, he seems to remind us: "For me, it's a symbol of his strength and kind of also his weakness" for all the ugly things in life that brought him to the surgery table. "This cross was given to me to say goodbye."

Is that what this is all about, then, that necessary, frightening, forever-and-forever good-bye? As a teenager, I used to get angry that my home, the childhood home I grew up in, would somehow outlive me. That when all was said and done, as I waved good-bye and good-bye to all my loved ones, and when my bones were lying in some grave, when my descendants would forget that I ever existed, the house would remain tall and standing. But even gold can outlast a house.

I don't know what it is about these stories and gold—my golden *YESENIA*—that makes me keep coming back, demanding maybe even a moral to the story, a nice, clean takeaway like one of Perrault's fairytales.

* * *

Part of the answer, I soon discovered, was far, far removed, in the beginning, before the second darkness enveloped the skies.

You'll stumble upon it among the long deceased inhabitants of San Antonio near today's central Philippines, who, in the fourteenth and fifteenth centuries, long before the Spanish King arrived, buried their dead in gold masks, one finely shaped sheet for the nose, the other for the eyes. A custom inherited from the southern Chinese, it was said to prevent evil spirits from entering the body.[78]

Across the water and crisscrossing islands, you'll unearth another clue buried deep within the ancient cemeteries of east Java in today's Indonesia: golden funerary masks from the tenth century. Just brush off the dry dirt and you'll see how they outline particular features of the face of the deceased—the eyes, and sometimes eyebrows, the nose, and the mouth—while others cover the entire face. Either way, these golden death masks helped guarantee "that the status and wealth of the deceased was acknowledged in the afterlife."[79]

But now, we're being pushed back again, farther, deeper... (Will you be able to pull us up from out of here?)

Another signpost—this time among the ancient indigenous

Quimbaya tribe of present-day Colombia, who reigned from 600-1100 AD, before the King's horses ever stepped foot upon her lands. Only the most elite of the Quimbayans would be buried in special golden masks, teeth filed flat, with nose ornaments, and large, hanging earrings finely hammered to reflect the shining sun's beams. If the eyes of the mask were closed, it was said that that the deceased was "no longer looking out into the world of the living, but instead looking inside into the spirit world."[80]

Hundreds of miles south, down across the Andes, around the same time as the Quimbaya, ruled the lords of Lambayeque in northern Peru. "Compulsive hoarders of gold," the Lambayeque also buried their prominent in elaborate, massive golden masks. And not just one. It was discovered that as many as five masks could be buried with the deceased, one attached to the head and the other four piled upon each other at their feet.[81]

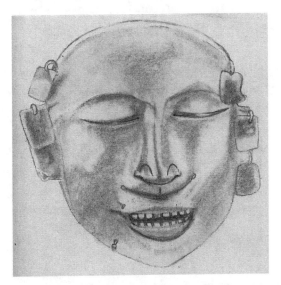

Funerary Death Mask Sketch by Karina Barragan.

Deeper, farther, and deeper...

The most famous of them all? The legendary gold burial "mask of Agamemnon," the mythical Greek hero immortalized in Homer's epic *Odyssey*. It hangs today in the National Archaeological Museum of crisis-hit Athens, a reminder of a different (and, yet, perhaps not too different?) Greece. And finally, the solid gold death mask of Pharoah Tutankhamun, "King Tut," the infamous Boy King who ruled Egypt at the age of 9. Buried in the Valley of the Kings, his death mask was his ticket to eternity, for the protective cobra, which would spit at his enemies, adorned his forehead. It would guide the Boy King on his long journey through the underworld.[82]

My God. Something large, larger than I ever expected, was at work here.

* * *

"Felicidades."

And I'm back at the gray, concrete stairs, staring wide-eyed at my golden *YESENIA*. But it's clear from the signposts now what she wants from me.

My golden necklace was no mere class-and-race-reductionist ritual, no simple social phenomenon. No, no, she was bigger, much bigger, than that. She was the first piece of my very own golden death mask that I would assemble over years and years to come. It would begin with her, and over time, I would slowly accumulate more and more little bits and pieces of the mask with the help of baptismal earrings here, a ring there. Enough, over the many years, to cover the mouth portion of my mask for my future burial.

I swear it's not a joke. Come closer and you can see for yourself.

She was my shot at getting the hell out of Hackensack, a testament to achieving ultimate economic and social immortality. But at what cost?

Chapter 4

At the Bottom of the Mine

"The gold at the end of the rainbow is ultimate happiness, but the gold at the bottom of the mine emerges from hell."
—Peter L. Bernstein, *The Power of Gold: A History of an Obsession*

June 20, 1810. Far away in the swampy, remote frontier town of Citará, New Granada (modern-day Quibdó, Colombia), once the central gold mining site of the illustrious Spanish Kingdom, an enslaved woman named Rosalia de los Santos purchased her freedom from her deceased master's inheritor for the rather large sum of 400 *pesos*. Like so many other enslaved Afro-Colombians on the Pacific Coast who worked those hellish gold mines under unimaginable circumstances, Rosalia offered 400 *pesos* worth of *gold dust* in exchange for her freedom.[83]

There it sat, Rosalia's future, piled up in an uneven mound of gold dust. Later that rainy day, perhaps right after receiving her own freedom papers, Rosalia would present another pile of gold dust, an undisclosed amount, a pile that would go towards purchasing the freedom of her enslaved daughter, Andrea. Standing before her deceased master's inheritor, Doña Gertrudis Pacheco, Rosalia stated that "as the mother of the *liberta* Andrea, a minor, I accept these [freedom papers]."[84] The fate of Rosalia, her daughter Andrea, and the countless living kin and future kin that would come after them would be sealed by those clean and refined piles of dark yellow gold dust.

Soon, the gold dust would acquire a new life of its own, from the gold mines or rivers of Chocó, into the hands of Rosalia, perhaps to an overseer, then to her master Don Antonio, carried off by a local merchant, by boat or overland if the rainy season wasn't especially heavy, eventually making its way to the port city of Cartagena, where it would be shipped off to London or Paris,[85] melted away, finally sent off to...

But would the gold dust remember Rosalia or Andrea? Or would it try to forget?

The long, hot hours at the river. The drops of sweat. The lash. The screams of terror. Streaming drops of blood. Dogs barking off in the distance. The hoarse laugh. The unbearable desire to forget everything and nothing at once. Is it possible? They're all there, trapped inside each gold dust particle, the countless hours beating at the earth inside the mine's tunnels, the endless panning in search of tiny golden nuggets hidden in the innumerable river streams.

Aunque mi amo me mate,
a la mina no voy.
Yo no quiero morirme
en un socavón.

(Though my master may kill me,
To the mine, I will not go.
I do not want to die
In the dark depths below.[86])

Would it try to forget its life buried within the ravine's rocks; its life at the bottom of the mine?

Tú eres su esclavo.
¡No, mi señor!
Tú eres su esclavo.
¡No, mi señor!
Y aunque me aten cadenas,
esclavo no soy.

(You are his slave.
No, my *señor*.
You are his slave.
No, my *señor*.
And although they've tied me up in chains,
I am not a slave.)

And there it is. For a moment, we can see Rosalia's coarse black hands running through a pile of soggy dirt, gray rocks, pebbles, combing her wooden pan in search of those golden pellets. Moving the pan in circles, back and forth, and back and forth. Would she find enough to fulfill her weekly quota, enough to please Don Antonio? Enough to place aside some for herself, of course, with the permission of Don Antonio (and sometimes without it), for Andrea? If we're quiet enough, maybe we can even hear Rosalia breathing…

But then, dogs barking off in the distance. Don Antonio is here. And she's gone.

* * *

"For every image of the past that is not recognized by the present as one of its own concerns threatens to disappear irretrievably."
—Walter Benjamin, *Theses on the Philosophy of History*

You can't miss it. You'll find it there, today, in the center of town, in Quibdó: the Cathedral of San Francisco de Asís. Tall and gray and not very attractive. A group of black workers are busy fixing the broken concrete stairs, endless tears of sweat rolling off their faces in the tropical Pacific coastal heat of Quibdó. They've been there for a few weeks now. My friends joke that the construction will never end.

A few feet away from us, Julieta, an Afro-Colombian

campesina woman sells delicious, grilled sweet *plátanos* with fresh cheese. Only fifty more cents for freshly squeezed orange juice. *"Riquísimo,"* she assures me, with a smile. Every morning, give or take, she sets up her stand in front of the cathedral. After a few visits at her stand, I learn that she, like so many of this city's residents, was forced to leave her village of Tadó, just south of Quibdó, a few years ago. (According to the Washington Office on Latin America, fifty-two percent of the residents of Quibdó are Afro-Colombians who were forcibly displaced from their lands in the last twenty years.[87] The sometimes combined, sometimes separate, work of the paramilitaries, guerrillas, drug lords, Colombian military...). A few feet away, there's another woman like Julieta also selling sweet plantains and cheese. And another woman across the street from her.

But at least Julieta has San Francisco de Asís. She gets up early enough to arrange her stand, before the others set up. She's the first stand that you see as you exit the church, the first vendor that the many, daily churchgoers pass by after the priest's sermons.

My favorite time of day to visit the church, though, is not during the two daily services, one at midday and one after 5 pm, but after them, after the end of the day, when it's just ever so slightly cooler and quiet, except for the occasional murmurings of the older, black women praying, rosaries clasped in their hands, with pictures of saints, sometimes photographs of lost loved ones, on their lap.

Walk a little further down the church's long nave, past the humming crowd of women, finally to the altar. Just beyond the altar, behind it, a mural depicts Chocó and Colombia's past. Or is it present?

Off, towards the bottom of the mural: a pile of golden dust. Could it be? Is that how Rosalia's pile of gold shimmered before Doña Pacheco? The gold sits there, a proud mound, poured out from the pan of an enslaved black man, who stands in front of a line of other enslaved men, women, and children. At the foot of the mound sits some Royal Official in a lavish chair, a *conquistador* standing next to him.

But hold on a second. Right next to the conquistador, behind the priest, stand three men who look like they could be alive now, right now, today, walking outside the church. In fact, I swear I saw one of them roaming around the pews. Three white men, one all dressed up in a blue suit and a red tie, pointing to the golden mound, an angry looking soldier in his uniform, and a stern-looking priest holding up a black cross above the crowd. What might the slick businessman be whispering in the priest's ear?

Mural inside the *Catedral San Francisco de Asis* in Quibdó, Colombia. Photo by author.

* * *

It was gold, of course, that offered an essential lifeline for the newly formed Christian Kingdom of Castile and Aragon, established by King Ferdinand II and Queen Isabella I in 1469. The gold would not only pay for their constant warfare throughout the Iberian Peninsula, Christendom, and beyond, but also forge their incipient global Empire.

By 1492, the same year Columbus set off in search of a quicker route to Asia on behalf of the Catholic monarchs, Ferdinand and Isabella had managed to re-conquer their own territories after successfully defeating the Muslim state of *Al-Andalus*, and they were on the search for more. The little bits of gold that Columbus brought back from Hispaniola a year later in 1493 were enough to get them on board, for they launched a second, more organized expedition from Cádiz in 1493.[88] By 1510, as the indigenous populations of the Caribbean were slowly being decimated by enslavement, disease, and other unspeakable violence, Ferdinand authorized 50 African slaves from the Iberian Peninsula to work the gold mines of Hispaniola.[89] A year later, King Ferdinand was said to have advised his armies with strict instructions: "Get gold, humanely if possible, but at all costs—*get gold.*"[90] (Perhaps knowing what was at stake, in 1554, the indigenous Araucanians of present-day Chile, ancestors of the Mapuches, allegedly captured the conquistador Pedro de Valdivia, who founded the city of Santiago, and "apparently put him to death by pouring molten gold down his throat."[91])

However, it was originally gold from West Africa, monopolized by the Portuguese in the fifteenth century, that really got the Iberians gold-crazy. Shuttling gold across the West African coast, the Portuguese even named the region *Mina de Ouro* ("The Gold Mine") or *Costa da Mina* ("The Gold Coast").[92] In the early 1500s, approximately 700 kilograms of gold were said to be moving from Africa to Portugal each year.[93] Thinking it a comparable site, tropical and expansive, with dark, native labor, Ferdinand and Isabella believed they would find similar treasures in their newly conquered territories in the so-called "New World."[94]

But, alas, this turned out to be far from the case. Although gold was certainly found throughout the Caribbean islands, it was not nearly the amount that the King and Queen dreamed of. In fact, by 1515, the gold placer deposits in Hispaniola had exhausted.[95] Soon, the King's conquistadors set off inland, into the mainland of the "New World" in search for more gold. The colonial region of *Tierra Firme*, which today covers the northern coast of Colombia, Venezuela, and Panama, was even renamed *Castilla del Oro* ("Golden Castile") in 1514 due to reports of gold. It was here on this territory of present-day Colombia that the infamous myth of *El Dorado*, the legendary "Lost City of Gold," appeared. Tales circulated of an ancient indigenous Chibcha ceremony at the sacred lake of Guatavita, not too far from today's capital of Bogotá, and reports of a "'king who went naked aboard a raft to make offerings, smeared all over with powdered gold from head to foot, gleaming like a ray of sun.'"[96] Although subsequent expeditions managed to drain the lake (even up to the twentieth century!) and some treasures were recovered, *El Dorado* was never found.

Gold also brought the Spanish to the once-illustrious *Tawantinsuyu*, the Incan Empire in present-day Peru in the 1520s and 1530s. By 1532, war broke out between the two heirs to the throne, brothers Huáscar and Atahualpa, while smallpox carried by the Spanish ravaged the indigenous Incans. Seeing the golden opportunity of a fissured, crumbling empire, and aided by military technology unknown to the Incans, the Spanish, led by Pizarro, began their conquest of the region that same year in 1532. Eventually, Huascar was killed, and the Spanish held Atahualpa ransom. What did they want in return? Gold. Lots and lots and lots of it. That is, they demanded that Atahualpa fill the entire dimensions of the room where he was held ransom (22 feet long, 17 feet broad and 9 feet high to be exact) with gold. From March to June 1533, over the course of four months, ancient golden plates, jewelry, cups, tiles from temples, and all sorts of monuments of Incan civilization were stacked up in that room and melted down before the conquistadors.[97] Although Atahualpa followed through with their request, he was nevertheless executed.

As time passed, the Spanish searched further and further for new golden exploits across the Americas. They soon found one in the hot, tropical Pacific lowlands of present-day Colombia: Rosalia's Chocó. Unlike Hispaniola or *Tawantinsuyu*, Chocó remained at the margins of the Spanish Empire for the first 150-200 years of colonial expansion. It was only after 1650 that the region emerged as a potential gold mining site.[98] Soon, word of the region's golden river streams and mines spread to miners and slave-owners. By 1704, the Spanish imported over 600 African slaves into Chocó. Twenty years later, an estimated 2,000 slaves were reported to be mining Chocó's gold. By the end of the century, there were 7,088 slaves in the region,[99] among them Rosalia's ancestors. Chained together in single file, Chocó's slaves were forced to travel from the slave port of Cartagena across hundreds of miles of rivers, jungles, swamps, before scaling the towering Andes. Once they passed through the Andes into Chocó's remote mining sites, they faced more hell, hunger and brutal enslavement.[100] It is no surprise that Chocó was often described at the time as the "demon's paradise," "the devil's sanctuary," and "the cradle of the abandoned."[101]

Chocó was not alone. Around the same time African slaves were being exported to the Colombian Pacific in the early 1700s, a gold rush began to form on the other side of the continent, in Minas Gerais in colonial Brazil. It is because of Minas Gerais that Brazilians know the eighteenth century as the *siglo do ouro*, the century of gold. By the end of that century, the population of Minas Gerais hit 400,000, 54% of which were slaves primarily from the shores of West Africa's Golden Coast, present-day Ghana. [102] "At all costs—*get gold*."

* * *

One of the essential attributes of gold, Peter L. Bernstein, author of *The Power of Gold: The History of an Obsession,* notes, was the fact that unlike any other product, gold was so malleable that it could take any shape or form and, moreover, it was imperishable. This means that all of the gold that has ever been mined in history is still circulating among us today. "In Cairo," Bernstein tempts us, "you will find a tooth bridge made of gold for an Egyptian 4500 years ago, its condition good enough to go into your mouth today."[103] Maybe even gold from the Pharaoh himself?

I wonder, then, whose gold it was that sat in my golden

YESENIA. Or the tooth of Valerio Novelli, a 56 year old ticket inspector on Rome's buses, who was forced to sell a gold tooth from his mouth for fast cash in 2011. As of August 2012, there were an estimated 28,000 cash-for-gold shops in Italy. "I can't get to the end of the month without running up debts," Novelli confessed, "I know I won't get much, but I need the money."[104]

Could there have been traces of the formerly enslaved Rosalia and Andrea's gold dust, their path to a fragile freedom, or even some of the Pharoah's gold in Novelli's mouth? What new anguishes would the future inheritors of Novelli's tooth, of Rosalia's gold dust, face in the years to come?

* * *

Gold is once again the sheriff in town across the Golden Coast. As *compro oro* shops pop up throughout the West, gold mines are multiplying in Ghana and across Africa in response to the crisis-induced spike in the price of gold.

But this time it's different. Instead of Portuguese and European merchants, Chinese speculators and local Ghanaian businessmen are providing the capital and tools necessary to cash in on this hot market. At one Ghanaian operation, miners, including children as young as four years old, work the mines for less than US $6 a day. Most mines are *galamsey*, meaning illegal, erected at such breakneck speed in such haphazard conditions with mining disasters exploding across the country.[105]

Such was the story of a mining site near Dunkwa-on-Offin in central Ghana, where a mine caved in, fatally sucking 150 miners into the ground in June 2010. Only 17 of the bodies were ever recovered. Local villagers soon fled the area when the ghosts of the miners began to haunt them. At night, they reported hearing drumming and chanting near the collapsed mine, as the ghosts moaned "I'm cold… I'm cold… I'm cold…"[106]

In April 2013, another mine collapsed in the Ghanaian town

of Kyekyewere, killing 16,[107] while more than 60 miners were killed at a gold mine in Darfur, Sudan (already ravaged by war) a month later.[108]

The gold rush has spread across the Atlantic, back to Colombia, where paramilitaries, drug warlords, and multinational corporations have reconquered the lands in pursuit of empire. You see, unlike cocaine and other 'illicit' drugs, warlords can legally fund their operations by selling gold.[109]

And that leaves people like my friend Francia Elena Márquez Mina, an Afro-Colombian artisan miner and land rights activist, in a tough situation. She is from La Toma, a small, gold mining community in Suárez, in northern Cauca, where her ancestors have been living and mining for more than 400 years. After the bloody Alta Naya massacre of 2001, not too far from La Toma, transnational mining corporations like AngloGold Ashanti slowly trickled into the region, eventually trying to take La Toma's mines. Since they started to fight back in 2009, her community has received 15 threats from paramilitary groups like the deadly *Aguilas Negras*. But this all goes way back, way back, Francia reminds us. "The racism that was used as a tool by capitalism to enslave our people," she tells us, "still exists today."

Perhaps Rosalia's gold dust can help us remember.

Chapter 5

Cash for a Golden Dawn

"As gold's unquenchable beauty shines like the sun, people have turned to it to protect themselves against the darkness ahead."

—Peter L. Bernstein, *The Power of Gold: A History of an Obsession*

It was a cold, wintery day in Athens, Greece in late 2011, when a "smartly dressed" middle-aged woman named Anna exited a cash-for-gold shop. 1,500 Euros clenched in her hand, she held the cash value of a pair of earrings and a gold watch that belonged to her husband, who refused to join her at the shop. "He couldn't do it, he was too embarrassed."[110]

Joining Anna on a similar mission, an unnamed 45-year-old Greek woman confessed the following on Twitter: "I opened up my cupboards and put emotion aside. I had a lot of gold jewelry and other items that I inherited from my mother and grand-mother and never wore," an exchange "which I'm hoping I'll soon forget."[111] At 55, Alexandria Verkokaki, whose family has owned a jewelry shop in downtown Athens since 1923, has also born witness to this abrupt financial-tectonic shift of recent years. "A lady came to me the other day crying because she needed to sell her gold jewels and didn't know what they were worth." Careful, though, he warned. "These are not poor folks. They are ordinary, middle-class Greeks: a woman with three kids who needs to sell her wedding jewelry just to send her kids to school."[112]

In Greece, the European capital of the Regime of Austerity, everyday people are selling off chunks of their gold; fragments of their death masks. With an unemployment rate of 27.6% as of

July 2013 (the highest figure in the history of the EU), and a youth unemployment rate of 65% as of May 2013 (also the highest in the EU), the pile of gold crucifixes, watches, necklaces, and baptismal gifts stashed behind the cash-for-gold shop counters across the country is growing with no clear end in sight. In Athens' infamous Syntagma Square, one of the central sites of mass resistance to the global neoliberal order, one pawnbroker noted that "two years ago, there were just five pawnshops in the area and now there are 25,"[113] whereas authorities have reported that 90% of the country's 224 officially registered pawnshops opened up shop in 2011, just a year after the Greek government accepted its first deathwish-austerity package.[114] As one in four businesses is forced to close across Greece,[115] the skeletal remains of yesterday's corner store, yesterday's neighborhood print-shop, gather dust as they swell late capitalism's urban graveyards. You can catch glimpses of these skeletons driving through the winding highways heading into Athens, as torn, decrepit billboards that haven't felt the touch of a human's hand in years, like unmarked tombstones with no known visitors, emerge from the rolling hills every hundred yards or so.

As you slowly make your way into the city, past the gray *polykatoikias* (imposing post-civil war apartment buildings that transformed Athens from "an elegant neo-classical city into an amorphic concrete mass"[116]), you'll find hints of this new golden sheriff in town. Seemingly endless leaflets stuffed into mailboxes, or slipped under apartment doors, under car windshield wipers, even in telephone booths (still in use in this part of the world), all offer the best deal crafted *just for you*. A poster in an Athens bus stop read "In Gold We Trust,"[117] (because in these times who else can you trust?)

But it's not just the littered mailboxes or car window screens that serve as real warning signs of certainly uncertain times ahead. It was said that the older generation of pawnbrokers used to work out of crowded basements or in "tucked-away apartments,"[118] hidden from plain sight. But now, the newest cash-for-gold shopkeepers are renting out storefronts in the city's most central locations, like Syntagma Square, announcing their presence with bright yellow signs proudly proclaiming *I BUY GOLD* and displays showcasing golden wedding rings and even gold teeth. "Transactions are not conducted in an aura of secrecy anymore," said one new cash-for-gold shop owner in Athens, "and they are no longer limited to the outcasts of society."[119]

And yet, despite the fact that cash-for-gold shops have expanded their clientele to those beyond the wretched of the earth, no matter where you go, all the shops are advised to be on *HIGH ALERT* for potentially stolen objects, especially jewelry; for it is impossible to trace such objects once they have been melted down into the **Outside a cash-for-** deep, dark recesses of a foundry. The **gold shop in Athens.** situation has gotten so bad, many say, that **Photo by Eliana.** thieves prowl around local neighborhoods looking for gold, and attack their targets in daylight even knowing that a family is present. "We were sitting on the front veranda chatting when they jumped from the roof to the back yard and got into the house," reported Mattheos Michelakakis, a 61-year old retiree living in a working-class neighborhood in Athens.[120] It's possible that the family's gold whisked away by the thieves is brewing in one of Athens' foundries, which tripled in number in 2011, with 10 operating in the

A cash-for-gold flyer in Athens. Photo by Eliana.

larger Athens area by the end of that year. Or maybe it has already been cooled down, hardened into compact golden bars, and smuggled off to Germany or Cyprus (two popular smuggling destinations), evading the country's taxes.[121] Perhaps an unnamed 70-year old pensioner heard Mattheos's story when she told a reporter, "I'd rather sell [my valuables] and use the money before some burglar grabs it all."[122]

And the craziest thing of it all is that the final frontiers of economic security—the bank, the personal safe, and the mattress—have been compromised. Fearing the bank would collapse in early 2012, 80 year old Andreas and Emilia Karabalis of the island of Lefkada withdrew their nearly 80,000 Euro savings and stored it away in their home. One night, "...we were sleeping. The two masked burglars came to our bed and tied us up. They hit us. They robbed us—they didn't leave anything, it was torture," said Emilia. "Our life," Andreas added, "is black now. They took our life's savings. We lost everything."[123] Across Greece, more and more people are moving their money out of the banks and into their cupboards or under their mattresses, often not informing anyone—not even their loved ones (who else is left to trust?)—about the new, secret location of their pile of Euros. On the island of Rhodes a family went so far as to tear down the walls of their recently deceased father's home, desperately searching for his secret stash, to no avail.

Who knows? Hidden beneath some kitchen floor tile, or perhaps lodged in an unassuming crevice, "future archaeologists may yet stumble on some of the buried treasure of the euro zone crisis of 2012."[124]

* * *

But with unemployment spiraling and a wild goose chase underway to pin down the Big Bad Guy responsible for this mess, instead of exchanging their gold for cash some Greeks are trading it in for a *Golden Dawn* — the fascist party with 18 seats in Parliament as of 2012 and known for launching bloody attacks on immigrants, queers, anarchists, and the Greek left.

Their sudden rise to power seems to have taken everyone by surprise. For the national elections in October 2009, they received 0.29% of the vote (19,624 votes), a still sizeable chunk of the population, but not enough to secure seats in Parliament. All that changed in 2012 after Golden Dawn slowly made inroads in local elections in 2010 (Nikos Michaloliakos, the founder and General Secretary of the party since their inception in 1983, won a seat on the City Council of Athens in 2010). In the wake of austerity's massive layoffs and unimaginable tax hikes on just about everything, Golden Dawn received a whopping 6.97% of the vote (*440,996 votes!*), earning them 21 seats in May 2012. This number dropped slightly (although not by much, all things considered) in the following emergency elections of June 2012, when Golden Dawn received 6.92% of the vote (426,025 votes), empowering them to 18 seats.[125]

And this was after one of their most out-spoken politicians, Ilias Kasidiaris, physically assaulted two left-wing members of Parliament on live television in early June![126] As hundreds of protestors took to the streets to denounce this act, a Facebook page praising his behavior accumulated 6,000 "likes" within 24 hours. "Blessed be the hand of Ilias Kasidiaris," the creators of the page wrote.[127] Eliana, a Greek friend and member of the Alpha Kappa anti-authoritarian movement, told me that recent national polls show that support for Golden Dawn is climbing up to 10%.[128]

One brisk afternoon, I was chatting with a Greek anarchist friend outside of *Nosotros*, Alpha Kappa's social center in the heart of Exarcheia, the infamous anarchist neighborhood of downtown Athens (and the site where police officers murdered the 15-year-old anarchist Alexandros Grigoropoulos, whose death launched the legendary riots of late 2008). On our way next-door to grab a kabob, he lamented that "we had no idea this would happen. They were a complete joke before." After a brief moment of silence, he pulled open the shop's door and added,

"We should've taken them more seriously."

Everywhere you go, I am told, Greeks are still trying to figure out how this xenophobic bad joke crystallized into today's fascist nightmare. How did this happen? Golden Dawn's official origin story begins in 1983, when the party's leader Nikos Michaloliakos launched the newspaper *Chrysi Avgi* ("Golden Dawn"), after years of participating in far right-wing groups, serving in the Greek army (from which he was eventually expelled), and spending a fair amount of time in jail where he met some of the leaders of the Greek military junta of 1967-1974. "We started in a Leninist way," Michaloliakos claimed, in a satirical tone. "We decided to issue a newspaper, *Golden Dawn*, and to build a party around it. Back in the 1980s, we flirted with all sorts of ideas of the interwar years, including National Socialism and fascism."[129] Indeed, harkening back to this time of terror, their symbol is a Greek meander, practically a Nazi swastika.

I had seen images of their symbol in news reports from Greece and in leaflets printed out by anti-fascist groups denouncing their presence, and I was happy to avoid any meaningful contact with the meander during my short visit to Athens—that is, until the tail end of my time there. Walking through the bustling, zigzagging streets in downtown Athens on my way to the Acropolis with my partner Mark, we passed by rows of small vendors selling all sorts of knickknacks and dusty souvenirs when a pair of shiny, dangling key-chains caught the corner of my eye. And there it was: the Golden Dawn meander staring back at me on a cheap, Made in China metal key-chain.

"Quick," I said to Mark, "Get the camera." In order not to make too much of a scene, and not bring too much unwanted attention given the shopkeeper's suspicious looks, I asked Mark to take a picture of my hand holding the popular Greek *nazar* necklace used to ward off the "evil eye," ironically hanging right next to the key-chains.

And right next to the meander was none other than Ilias

Kasidiaris! The same politician-thug I mentioned earlier who physically assaulted two female members of Greek Parliament on live television. In the photo, the face of the Nikos Michaloliakos, Golden Dawn's leader and founder, peaks out from under Kasidiaris, as if eerily descending off into the distance while a new young generation of fascists rises to the occasion. That evening, we brought the picture back to our comrades at *Nosotros* who were planning a large, anti-fascist demonstration a few days later. They had never seen this kind of mass-produced, fascist merchandise before. "Where did you see this?" one of them asked me sternly. We tried to explain the general location of the shop. I'm not sure what eventually happened.

Nevertheless, although Golden Dawn officially launched in the 1980s, it wasn't until the 1990s when real organizing and political activity began to materialize, especially in 1993 when they began to demonstrate against nationalist mobilizations in neighboring Macedonia. "...By the 1990s, we had settled the ideological issues and positioned ourselves in favour of popular nationalism,"[130] asserted Michaloliakos. By that time, in the 1990s, they were well known throughout Greece for disseminating Nazi propaganda and violently attacking immigrants and leftists. But in 2010, as the economic crisis was escalating, Golden Dawn slowly began to creep its way into mainstream political life. "In 2010, we said we should take over Athens in order to spread the message to the rest of Greece, as well," Michaloliakos said, "We strategically participated in this election for this reason. We knew we would succeed."[131]

How exactly would they succeed and save Greece from the disaster ahead? The party's statutes offer a brief but chilling answer. In it, they declare that the party's mission is to organize "'against the demographic alteration, through the millions of illegal immigrants, and the dissolution of Greek society, which is systematically pursued by the parties of the establishment of the so-called Left.'"[132] And similar to the Colombian paramilitaries who launch limpiezas (Spanish for "cleansings") meant "to wipe out and kill defenseless people"[133] including union organizers, the homeless, homosexuals, and anyone deemed 'undesirable' to the 'fabric of society,' Golden Dawn's members have initiated 'cleansing' operations throughout Athens and Greece, "vigilante-type activities aiming to clear Athenian neighborhoods of foreigners and to protect citizens from crime."[134]

Although Golden Dawn had been attacking immigrants and leftists long before their ascent to power, most argue that the far-right violence reached a new level of intensity in mid-May 2011. As thousands of young Spaniards started to occupy their town squares launching the 15M (indignado) movement which would soon spread to Athens' Syntagma Square, hundreds of miles away a crowd of nearly five hundred Greeks, including many members of Golden Dawn, began to indiscriminately attack immigrants in broad daylight, "chasing them through the streets, dragging them off buses, beating and stabbing them."[135]

Nineteen immigrants and six Greeks were injured, and many of their shops were destroyed.[136]

The horror stories, however, did not stop there. On August 5, 2011, a 25-year old Afghan refugee named Maria was attacked alongside her husband in broad daylight. Standing near the Attiki metro station in Athens, two men on a motorcycle hit her with a wooden club as they sped by. "I held my hand in front of my head when something hit my hand ... My hand was hurt severely ... It was injured so deeply that you could see the bone."[137] Just a month later, in September of 2011, Ali Rahimi, a 27-year old Afghan asylum seeker, along with two of his friends, were attacked by a large group outside an apartment building in Agios Panteleimonas, a small town in western Greece. Rahimi suffered five stab wounds to his torso. "We came from so far away and it is so easy to get killed here," he said.[138] A few weeks later, in October 2011, near the Agios Panteleimonas church in Athens, a 20-year old Somali woman named Mina Ahmad, who was six months pregnant at the time, was walking with her infant daughter when she was approached by a group of men. "They asked me first, 'Where are you from?' I said Somalia. When I answered they tried to take my daughter away ... They hit me on the head with a wooden stick ... I fell down bleeding. When I fell down and they saw I was bleeding they ran away. My daughter was crying. All the people [around at the time of the attack] they were watching but nobody helped me. I didn't go to the hospital ... It didn't matter if I was hurt. I just thought about the baby and my daughter."[139] Many victims don't turn to the police because they fear deportation or retaliation, or also because they simply cannot afford it. As a recent Human Rights Watch report stated, "three victims who insisted that they wished to pursue a case were told they would have to pay a 100 Euro fee (US $125) instituted in late 2010 to discourage frivolous criminal complaints."[140]

The situation didn't subside the following year. In June of

2012, a week after Golden Dawn got elected to Parliament, 50 party members rode their motorcycles through the streets of Nikaia, a neighborhood west of Athens with a large immigrant community, armed with large, wooden poles. According to Mohammed Irfan, a Pakistani immigrant and owner of a hair-salon and two other stores in the neighborhood, the party members came by shouting: "'You're the cause of Greece's problems. You have seven days to close or we'll burn your shop— and we'll burn you."[141] In September, one month before Greece's 20th general strike since the first austerity measures were passed in 2011, Golden Dawn politicians George Germenis, Elias Panagiotaros and Constantinos Barbarousis led a group of party members to attack immigrant vendors in the coastal towns of Rafina and Mesologgi, using the poles of their Greek flags to destroy their stalls.[142] Meanwhile, a flyer taped onto a telephone by a vigilante group, Citizens of Athens, announced their campaign to immigrants passing by, in English:

RETURN TO YOUR COUNTRY NOW ... YOU ARE NOT WANTED HERE
More than 90% of Greek people, want you to go away, and never come back and is angry with you and hate you for insulting our dignity.
We are angry with this government and all politicians that brought you and support you and defend you **AND WE ARE DETERMINED TO PUNISH THEM AND YOU.**
From now on, we will take every necessary action in order to force you and the TRAITORS-POLITICIANS that help you – GET OUT OF THIS COUNTRY...

YOU HAVE NO FUTURE IN GREECE ... GO HOME NOW CITIZENS OF ATHENS[143]

2013 wasn't any different. In the early morning hours of January

16, a 27-year old Pakistani man, Shehzad Luqman, was riding his bicycle on his way to work when two men who claimed he was 'blocking' their way murdered him. Born in 1986, the same year I was born, Shehzad had been living and working in Greece for six years. The relatives he was living with even showed reporters his 'pink card,' proving that Shehzad had legal work papers. For a daily wage of 20 Euros, Shehzad labored in a farmers' market, loading crates of oranges and potatoes day in and day out. He sent back most of his money to Pakistan to support his eight siblings who remained there. Alongside knives, switchblades, one set of brass knuckles, and two baseball bats, police officers found 50 Golden Dawn leaflets in the apartment of the murderers.[144] A few days later, on January 19, nearly 5,000 pro-immigrant and anti-fascist demonstrators took to the streets of Athens to denounce his murder.[145]

The circumstances have gotten so bad that Yunus Mohammadi, the president of an association of Afghans in Greece, has started to show new immigrants a map of Athens with red lines around the areas they need to avoid. "This is exactly what I used to do in Afghanistan with the Red Cross about places people shouldn't go because of fighting ... And here I am doing the same thing in a European country."[146]

And it's not *just* immigrants and asylum seekers that Golden Dawn is targeting: it's really *any* damn non-white person, or any person of color. In 2012, a Korean backpacker Hyun Young Jung traveling through Athens was approached by a man in uniform who demanded his ID. After handing over his passport, he asked the man to show his police ID. Instead, Jung was punched in the face and dragged to the nearest police station, where he realized he was under arrest. At the station, he was punched and attacked several more times by police officers. That summer, police officers also attacked a Nigerian-American tourist, Christian Ukwuorji, who was visiting Greece on vacation with his family. Although he also showed his passport, he was dragged to the police station where he was so horribly beaten that he passed out and woke up in a hospital.[147] The US State Department even issued a warning in November of 2012 to American tourists visiting Greece:

> There has been a rise in unprovoked harassment and violent attacks against persons who, because of their complexion, are perceived to be foreign migrants. US citizens most at risk are those of African, Asian, Hispanic, or Middle Eastern descent. Travelers are urged to exercise caution, especially in the immediate vicinity of Omonia Square from sunset to sunrise. Travelers should avoid Exarchia Square and its immediate vicinity at all times. The US Embassy has confirmed reports of US African-American citizens detained by police authorities conducting sweeps for illegal immigrants in Athens.[148]

(And the most ironic part of it all, for me, a short, brown-skinned Latina woman, was that the anarchist neighborhood of Exarcheia was really the only place I felt any sliver of security in Athens, as it is a main place where many local anti-fascist and anti-racist organizers gather together and look out for each other).

Graffiti in Exarcheia.
Photo by Mark Bray.

Why not, one may ask, just call the cops and clean up house? That could surely do the trick, right? Of course, there are some "bad apples" here and there (the ad-nauseam script of the NYPD), but with some tough police pressure on these Golden Dawn thugs, couldn't we just call it a day?

The problem is that the line between the two is blurring more and more, again, similar to the relationship between paramilitaries and the state in Colombia. In 2012, a senior Greek police officer who spoke to the *Guardian* on the condition of anonymity said that Golden Dawn has 'infiltrated' the police at various levels. The authorities "had been fully aware of the activities of Golden Dawn for several years, with the National Intelligence Service and other security agencies monitoring it closely. The officer claimed police chiefs had had the opportunity to isolate and remove these small 'pockets of fascism' in the force but decided not to. The state, he said, wanted to keep the fascist elements 'in reserve' and use them for its own purposes."[149] A few months after this confession, 15 anti-fascist activists who had organized a massive, anti-fascist motorcycle patrol in support of one of Athens' immigrant neighborhoods were arrested and subjected to Abu Ghraib-style torture by the police officers, who threatened to give their home addresses to Golden Dawn.[150] (But could it be any surprise, this not-so-secret marriage between the crumbling Greek state and the ascending Golden Dawn? I mean, this is in a country where the current Prime Minister, Antonis Samaras, repeatedly rails against the supposed "invasion" of "illegal immigrants.")

Golden Dawn hasn't just crept into the police headquarters. They've entered the country's schools, communities, and hospitals (or were they there were all along?). In 2012, at a local high school in Athens, several male students sympathetic to Golden Dawn left their classrooms to beat up a dark-skinned mailman passing by the school.[151] (But I shouldn't neglect to mention that thousands of high school students in Athens have also organized several anti-fascist demonstrations since 2011).

It's not just the high schools that Golden Dawn is after: in early 2013, they announced plans to open up nursery schools to teach "Greek ideals," after they received complaints that young Greeks were reading textbooks that were too pro-Jewish.[152] Across Greece, ordinary people are lining up to receive free bags of pasta and potatoes from Golden Dawn party volunteers, that is, as long as they show their identity papers.[153] They've launched Greek-only blood-drives and even started an organization called "Doctors With Borders," which offers free consultations for ethnic Greeks.[154]

So why instead of cash are some Greeks exchanging their gold, their promise in the future, for a bloody Golden Dawn? An unnamed Greek woman offered her thoughts on the matter: "Nature hates vacuums and Golden Dawn is just filling a vacuum that no other party is addressing."[155] Like so many poor Colombians who support the paramilitaries "because the Colombian state cannot protect them from anything,"[156] Golden Dawn offers, the same woman notes, "'little people' a sense that they can survive, that they are safe in their own homes."[157]

But who exactly are the 'little people' and who's home are we in? I can't imagine that she's talking about Shehzad Luqman (rest in power) or Mina Ahmad's cramped apartment, or even the storage space located above the toilet of a crowded apartment where a young Somali couple lives in central Athens.[158] Or the studio of anti-fascist rapper Pavlos Fyssas, aka Killah P, whose murder at the hand of Golden Dawn members in September 2013 sparked, perhaps for the first time, a concerted backlash against Golden Dawn.[159] Hell, at this point, it's not even the home of Andreas and Emilia Karabalis, the elderly couple living on the island of Lefkada who lost their life savings at the hands of burglars. So where on earth do we go from here?

"It is between myth and fear," writes Nikos Dimou, "that the Greeks live and create."[160]

* * *

Yet, unlike any other place in the world (even Spain, the headquarters of this gold rush), Greece's mushrooming cash-for-gold shops have become the physical target of Greek dissidents. In the city of Chalkida, for example, in southern Greece, the

"Network of tangible solidarity and resistance" disseminated posters in mid-November 2012 targeting the cash-for-gold shops littering the city's streets:

Image from "Occupied London: From the Greek Streets,"
November 14, 2012.

"I Buy gold.
Jewelry, teeth, wedding rings,
Badges, baptism crosses, relics,
Memories, belongings and dignity.
IN DEROGATORILY LOW PRICES.
Because I know you are desperate.
I know you can't afford your housing tax,
Your kid's tuition, your medicine, your food.
I know that you are in despair and that you don't know
How to resist, that you're scared.
I know, therefore, that you'll take whatever I give you,
And that you'll even thank me on top.
Yesterday a black-marketeer,
Today a pawnbroker,
Always filth."

There was another attack later that month in Athens, this time against a pawnshop in the neighborhood of Kato Petralona. The attackers trashed the storefront leaving behind leaflets proclaiming, "*Mavragorites*, out of our neighborhoods; not an inch of land to the loan sharks." In Greece, this term, *mavragorites*, refers to the black marketers who sold staple goods at high prices during the Nazi occupation of Greece from 1940-1944. "All those who see our poverty and impoverishment as an opportunity to make a quick buck," they warn, "will face the wrath of the revolted. We stand side by side to one another. Solidarity is the weapon of the people."[161] A month earlier, in early October 2012, attackers smashed the windows of a cash-for-gold shop in Igoumenitsa, in northwestern Greece, two hundred miles from Athens.[162] And then, in early March of 2013, there were rumors of a "coordinated attack" against three cash-for-gold shops in the port city of Volos in central Greece.

Volos. You may have come across this quaint city's name while perusing the safe pages of the *Guardian* or the *New York Times*, for the city has become famous in recent years due to the popularity of its new alternative economy, a dynamic bartering system. Taking a stroll through the colorful outdoor markets of Volos, you'll see locals selling oranges, candles, or napkins in exchange for olive oil, cheese, and even yoga lessons. "I can get language classes or computer lessons in return," noted Stavros Ntentos, who sells children's underwear at his stall. Perhaps reading the collective mind of so many Greeks, a man named Tasos, who sells vegetables at one of the markets, added, "We have reached the bottom of our lives and we now have to think in a different way."[163]

But in all of these stories coming out of Volos, one cannot help but be struck by reports of an overwhelming sense of freedom, if only temporarily, in being able to leave one's wallet at home. Have you ever tried it? Theodoros Mavridis, an unemployed electrician (and co-founder of this bartering network in Volos), said he felt such a thrill the first time he purchased eggs, milk, and jam at one of these outdoor markets: "I felt liberated, I felt free for the first time ... I instinctively reached into my pocket, but there was no need."[164]

Like the pile of glass shards outside of the cash-for-gold storefronts, the growing mass of people suddenly ceasing to reach into their pockets has become a new landscape of our times in this corner of the world.

* * *

Meanwhile, in northern Greece, the Greek State wants their share of the pot of gold by establishing a gold mining project led by the Canadian Eldorado Gold Corporation, named after the legendary "Lost City of Gold." Due to open in 2015, it is estimated that almost a gram of gold can be found in every ton of soil within a nearly 317 thousand square foot area.[165] Legend even has it that Alexander the Great, the man himself, mined for gold here.[166] ("Whenever a Greek looks at himself," writes Nikou Damos, "he sees either Alexander the Great ... or (at least) Onassis. Never Karaghiozis [comic puppet character from the Greek popular shadow theater].")[167]

But before unearthing the gold of the mountainside, Eldorado must clear out a previously protected natural forest reserve, followed by the unavoidable release of arsenic, cadmium, and all sorts of chemicals necessary for the refinement process.[168] Local residents remember the days in the not-so-distant past when the chemicals would stream down to the sea and sometimes turn it yellow. It was only ten years ago when Greece's highest courts banned mining in the region, claiming that environmental devastation would outweigh any monetary incentives.[169]

But ten might as well be fifty years—for these are different times and this is a different Greece. (Or is it any different?)

Despite the heavy propaganda in favor of the mining project, hundreds and thousands have demonstrated across Greece, from the local villages in Halkidiki, the site of the mine, to Thessaloniki, the nearest major city, to Syntagma Square in Athens. "We want the land, the water and the trees, not a golden tomb!" shouted villagers at one of the demonstrations,[170] while a banner was hung in Halkidiki proclaiming: "Many loved gold, no one loved cancer."[171] In October of 2012, 21 villagers were violently arrested at a protest against the mine, including a 62-year old woman named Rania Ververidis who was "ordered out of her car and told to kneel. At that point, she said, a police officer had stomped on her ankle. She was still limping three weeks later."[172] Months later, in February of 2013, "dozens of masked intruders" attacked the mining site with petrol bombs, setting fire to the machinery and company vehicles.[173]

Reading like a communiqué from rural Colombia, a statement by the Committees Against Gold Mining in Halkidiki from February 21, 2013 declares: "...the absurdity that is called 'development' creates temporary jobs while permanently destroying thousands of others. The economy of Halkidiki is based on tourism, agriculture, livestock, fisheries and apiculture [beekeeping], activities that will be, literally, vanished from the presumed development investment."[174]

Whatever the future of Halkidki, the new mining project has split the region into two distinct camps, even at times pitting family members each other. It is said that those who live near the sea more often oppose the project, while those who live in the interior, in the hills where work is hard to come by, tend to support it.[175]

But surely the officials remember the fate of Jason and Medea? Not too far from Eldorado's gold pits, Jason searched for the magical Golden Fleece he needed to regain his father's kingdom. And yes, he managed to acquire it but only with the help of the beautiful princess Medea. But not long after he held the glimmering fleece in his hands did he forget about Medea, and soon abandoned her and their children for another breath-taking woman. Ultimately, not all the gold in the world could protect Jason's sons from Medea's vengeance, for she murdered them and flew off in a chariot pulled by fire-breathing dragons.

Let us hope that the children of Greece do not suffer the same fate.

The End: Flesh and Bone

"13. The work is the death mask of its conception."
–Walter Benjamin, "Post No Bills: The Writer's Technique in Thirteen Theses"

But, really, how different is the cash-for-gold shop from the myriad of other physical remnants of this ongoing economic catastrophe, the rapidly changing physical landscapes of austerity that are surgically whittling down cities, small towns, schools, and hospitals to their flesh and brittle, bare bones?

As the cash-for-gold shops reign over the Kingdom of Austerity, homes owned and rented by poor and working-class people are being quickly emptied, locked, and stripped down under the strict orders of robo-call bank officials and their trusted police cronies. In cities like Detroit, already gravely hit and where banks foreclosed on more than 100,000 homes from 2000 to 2012, one of the highest in the nation, the eviction rate "was so high that the city hired additional workers—whom residents dubbed 'Blackwater bailiffs'—to keep pace."[176] Blackwater, of course, referring to the private military company used by the US government in Iraq and throughout the Middle East, slowly bringing the war home...

"On the East Side of the city," writes Laura Gottesdiener, who documented the vibrant housing justice and occupation struggles in Detroit and other cities over the past few years, "entire square miles are fully vacant except for the occasional deer or fox scampering through the shells of old industrial plants. Overhead, lazy blimps advertise scrap metal to no one. One sign, erected on Eight Mile Road, reads: WARNING! THIS CITY IS INFESTED BY CRACKHEADS. SECURE YOUR BELONGINGS AND PRAY FOR YOUR LIFE. YOUR LEGISLATORS WON'T PROTECT YOU."[177]

| Graphic shared widely throughout social networking sites during the heydays of Occupy Wall Street. | An abandoned home adorned with the marks of an Occupy Wall Street anti-foreclosure action in East New York, December 2011. Photo by Joe Lustri. |

Our flashy row of cash-for-gold shops, alongside the eerie patchwork of abandoned and at long last occupied houses, is later joined by a stream of shutdown hospitals and schools, whose long corridors and wards echo in silence, except for the occasional mouse or fox who finds a new home in this late capitalist wreckage. In Ireland, hospitals began to shut down some wards at the end of 2012, forcing patients home for the weekend as health services faced cuts of US $163 million across services.[178] In Greece, in August and September of 2013, doctors and hospital staff were on strike for three days in protest against massive lay-offs and shutting-down of hospitals.[179] And let's not forget about the now quiet hallways and cafeterias of the 47 schools that were closed in Chicago, almost all in poor African-American and Latino neighborhoods, or the 23 shutdown schools in Philadelphia, representing nearly 10% of the city's total. Meanwhile, in Philadelphia, officials are spending $400 billion to build a prison, the second-most-expensive facility ever constructed in the state of Pennsylvania.[180]

Welcome to the MAKE-BELIEVE-NOT-SO-MAKE-BELIEVE Kingdom of Austerity, complete with a littering of cash-for-gold shops, shiny new prisons, rows of foreclosed homes, and abandoned hospitals and schools!

And if you walk just a little further beyond the Kingdom's limits, you'll find its ever-expanding cemetery, one of the hottest businesses in town, that is, after the cash-for-gold shop. According to economist David Stuckler and physician Sanjay Basu, more than 10,000 people have committed suicide across Europe and the United States since governments introduced austerity.[181] Fresh, new mounds of dirt are piled up every hour of every day. On April 4, 2012, a 77-year old retired Greek pharmacist named Dimitris Christoulas was buried here after he shot himself near the Parliament in Athens. Speaking of her father at his funeral, his daughter Emi said:

> You found it unacceptable that they were killing our freedom, our democracy, our dignity. You found it unacceptable as they tightened the harsh noose of economic austerity and apartheid around us, to the unacceptable act of surrendering our independence and the keys to the country. It was unacceptable to you that Greece did not acknowledge its children and its children did not recognize their own country. You found the bestiality of capitalism unacceptable, that it infiltrated our lives and no one tried to stop it. Then, you made your decision to become the fear, the death, the memory, the sorrow of our ruined lives.[182]

Maybe that's what the cash-for-gold shop, in the end, can teach us. To stop the craziness of the golden death mask logic, once and for all, to visualize a future beyond capitalism and all its nastiness. To try, for a moment to make it all stop—"no one tried to stop it"—to pull the emergency brake, to make all the pain go away.

* * *

Thinking back about his life growing up in devastated Hiroshima after the atomic bomb, the legendary manga artist Keiji Nakazawa wrote: "Day after day American soldiers came for 'atomic tourism' from the US bases at Iwakuni and Kure, and atomic orphans sold them the skulls of bomb victims as mementos. I witnessed that many times near the Dome. But I couldn't blame the orphans struggling to survive. They even stole the countless weather-beaten skulls that had been collected by residents in the burned-out waste and placed in a grave for those with no survivors. They extracted the gold teeth and traded the gold for cash. On the surface, Hiroshima was being swaddled in beautiful clothing, but beneath the surface, the ugly struggle for survival went on."[183]

Perhaps then, listening to Nakazawa, we should try to understand the *compro oro* pawnshop as painshop. Here, people mutilate themselves for cash. Here, people sell off their death masks for the immediate. There, inside the painshop, *"the ugly struggle for survival went on."*

But you'll have to see it for yourself—whether it's at *Puerta del Sol*, or anywhere else. And quick, too, before there's no more gold to sell and even the *compro oro* shops must shut down. Who knows? One day, when the going gets tough, you too might come across a piece of my golden *YESENIA* (or maybe even Rosalia's gold dust, or Valerio's tooth) once it's finally time to assemble your own death mask. My only request is that you remember "what has been sold/[is] not strictly made of stone ... just remember that it's flesh and bone."[184]

Endnotes

1   Daniel Miller, *Stuff* (Cambridge, UK: Polity, 2010), 54.

2   Ibid., 50.

3   Fernando Pérez Ávila, "La ciudad del compro oro," *El Diario de Sevilla*, December 3, 2012, http://www.diariodese villa.es/sevilla/detail.php?id=1411783.

4   "El oro, un valor en alza para España," *RT*, September 7, 2011, http://actualidad.rt.com/economia/view/32383-El-oro,- un-valor-en-alza-para-España.

5   Dave Stelfox, "How the corrala movement is occupying Spain," *The Guardian*, March 4, 2013, http://www. guardian.co.uk/world/2013/mar/04/corrala-movement- occupying-spain.

6   Stanley G. Payne, *The Franco Regime, 1936-1975* (Madison, Wis.: University of Wisconsin Press, 1987), 620.

7   Stelfox, "How the corrala movement is occupying Spain."

8   Giles Tremlett, "Spain: the pain of austerity deepens," *The Guardian*, January 1, 2013, http://www.guardian.co.uk /world/2013/jan/01/spain-pain-austerity-deepens.

9   Suzanne Daley, "Spain Recoils as Its Hungry Forage Trash Bins for a Next Meal," *The New York Times*, September 24, 2012, http://www.nytimes.com/2012/09/25/world/europe/ hunger-on-the-rise-in-spain.html?pagewanted=all.

10 Stelfox, "How the corrala movement is occupying Spain."

11 Ibid.

12 Ibid., http://www.theguardian.com/world/gallery/2013/ma r/04/spanish-corralas-in-pictures#/?picture=404874837 &index=4.

13 "Stop Deshaucios atribuye a un proceso de desahucio el suicidio de un hombre en Basauri," *Naiz*, February 12, 2013, http://www.naiz.info/es/actualidad/noticia/20130212/stop- desahucios-atribuye-a-un-desahucio-el-suicidio-de-un-

hombre-en-basauri.

14 "Denuncian un nuevo suicidio por deshaucio en Vizcaya," *Diario Información*, February 12, 2013, http://www.diarioinformacion.com/sucesos/2013/02/12/denuncian-nuevo-suicidio-desahucio-vizcaya/1343019.html.

15 "Evicted retired couple commits suicide as Spain debates reform," *The Raw Story*, February 12, 2013, http://www.rawstory.com/rs/2013/02/12/evicted-retired-couple-commits-suicide-as-spain-debates-reform/.

16 "4 commit suicide in Spain over evictions as EU struggles with unemployment," *RT News*, February 14, 2013, http://rt.com/news/spain-eviction-suicide-homeless-184/.

17 Agustino Fontevecchia, "Spanish Woman Commits Suicide As Foreclosure Agents Walk Into Her Apartment," *Forbes*, November 9, 2012, http://www.forbes.com/sites/afontevecchia/2012/11/09/spanish-woman-commits-suicide-as-foreclosure-agents-walk-into-her-apartment/.

18 "'Homicide not suicide': Spain facing 'humanitarian' crisis over evictions," *RT News*, November 22, 2012, http://rt.com/news/spain-evictions-debt-crisis-302/.

19 Pedro Cerrada, "Un hombre aparece ahorcado en la calle diez días después de ser desahuciado en Alicante," *Diario Información*, April 13, 2013, http://www.diarioinformacion.com/sucesos/2013/04/13/hombre-aparece-ahorcado-calle-diez-dias-despues-desahuciado-alicante/1362872.html.

20 Daley, "Spain Recoils as Its Hungry Forage Trash Bins for a Next Meal."

21 Ibid.

22 Ibid.

23 David González, "La compraventa de oro y otros metales preciosos genera más de 90 millones de euros al mes," *ARN Digital*, July 26, 2012, http://www.arndigital.com/economia/noticias/3070/la-compraventa-de-oro-y-otros-

metales-preciosos-genera-mas-de-90-millones-de-euros-almes/.

24   Maria Martin, "Fiebre del oro en la Puerta del Sol," *El País*, July 18, 2010, http://elpais.com/diario/2010/07/18/madrid/1279452264_850215.html.

25   Patricia Hermida, "Galicia abrió más de 100 locales para comprar oro desde la crisis," *El Correo Gallego*, September 15, 2011, http://www.elcorreogallego.es/galicia/ecg/galicia-abrio-100-locales-comprar-oro-crisis/idEdicion-2011-09-15/idNoticia-700421/.

26   Dan Bilefsky, "Hard Times in Spain Force Feuding Couples to Delay Divorce," *The New York Times*, December 17, 2012, http://www.nytimes.com/2012/12/18/world/europe/hard-times-in-spain-force-feuding-couples-to-delay-divorce.html?_r=0.

27   "Las tiendas de compraventa de oro se triplican en un año," *ABC*, August 14, 2010, http://www.abc.es/20100814/comunidad-castillaleon/tiendas-compraventa-triplican-20100814.html.

28   Pérez Ávila, "La ciudad del compro oro."

29   "El oro, un valor en alza para España," *RT News*, September 7, 2011, http://actualidad.rt.com/economia/view/32383-El-oro,-un-valor-en-alza-para-España.

30   Lola Sampedro, "Así funciona el negocio del oro," *El Mundo*, February 23, 2011, http://www.elmundo.es/elmundo/2011/02/23/baleares/1298457914.html.

31   Guy Hedgecoe, "Gold dealers provide needed cash in struggling Spain," *The Global Post*, May 10, 2011, http://www.globalpost.com/dispatch/news/regions/europe/spain/110509/cash-for-gold-spain.

32   Andrew Moran, "Gold ATM machine activated in China, 2000 more to be installed," *Digital Journal*, September 28, 2011, http://digitaljournal.com/article/312073.

33   Dan Hancox, "The Streets of Spain," *The New Inquiry*,

November 20, 2012, http://thenewinquiry.com/essays/the-streets-of-spain/.

34 "El refugio del oro, en España," *Antena3.com*, November 5, 2012, http://www.antena3.com/programas/equipo-investigacion/noticias/refugio-oro-espana_2012110400012.html.

35 Russell Maddicks and Hilary Dunsterville Branch, *Venezuela: The Bradt Travel Guide* (Chalfont St. Petersburg: Bradt Travel Guide, 2011), 358.

36 Elizabeth Gackstetter Nichols and Kimberly J. Morse, *Venezuela* (Santa Barbara, California: ABC-CLIO, 2010), 188-189.

37 As quoted by Mark Fisher in *Capitalist Realism: Is There No Alternative?* (Winchester, UK: Zero Books, 2009).

38 Esther Cuesta, "'We're Better Off Outside Our Country': Diasporic Ecuadorian Women in Spain Since the Mid-1990s," in *Journal of Developing Societies* 23, 113 (2007): 118.

39 Brian Gratton, "Ecuadorians in the United States and Spain: History, Gender, and Niche Formation," in *Journal of Ethnic and Migration Studies* 33, 4 (May 2007): 586.

40 Mary Pool and Jelena Kopanja, "Reverse Migration: Ecuador Lures Immigrants Back Home from U.S. and Spain," *Feet in 2 Worlds*, September 4, 2009: http://feet in2worlds.wordpress.com/2009/09/04/reverse-migration-ecuador-lures-immigrants-back-home-from-u-s-and-spain/#more-9087

41 González, "La compraventa de oro y otros metales preciosos genera más de 90 millones de euros al mes."

42 Simon Romero, "Cocaine Wars Make Port Colombia's Deadliest City," *The New York Times*, May 22, 2007, http://www.nytimes.com/2007/05/22/world/americas/22colombia.html?pagewanted=all.

43 For more, see the company's website at http://www.asturgold.com/s/Home.asp.

44 "El refugio del oro, en España," *Antena3.com*, November 5,

2012, http://www.antena3.com/programas/equipo-investigacion/noticias/refugio-oro-espana_2012110400012.html.

45   To be clear, the pawnshop as a historic phenomenon is distinct from collateral-based lending, which has existed since biblical times. For example, in the Old Testament, there are references to receiving clothing as pledge of repayment. However, as Natalia Buier has pointed out, the relationship between the pawnshop and the cash-for-gold shop itself may not be so clear cut, as "cash for gold shops might be seen as qualitatively distinct from pawn shops on account of the properties of gold as a commodity the use value of which is secondary (and in that sense distinct from many other commodity circulating through pawn shops)" (personal communication via email, January 5, 2014).

46   T.S. Whelan, *The Pawnshop in China* (Ann Arbor: Center for Chinese Studies, University of Michigan, 1979), 1.

47   Ibid., 2.

48   Ibid., 3.

49   Ibid., 4.

50   Kenneth Hudson, *Pawnbroking: An Aspect of British Social History* (London: Bodley Head, 1982), 22.

51   Ibid., 24; Wendy Woloson, *In Hock: Pawning in America from Independence through the Great Depression* (Chicago: University of Chicago Press, 2009), 7-8.

52   Woloson, *In Hock: Pawning in America*, 7.

53   Irina Chekhovskich and Heiko Schrader, "The History of Pawnshops in Russia: A Documentation," Working Paper No. 325, Universität Bielefeld, Sociology of Development Research Centre, 2.

54   Azila Abdul-Razak, "Economic and Religious Significance of the Islamic and Conventional Pawnbroking in Malaysia: Behavioural and Perception Analysis," Durham theses, Durham University (2011), 33; Marieke Bos, Susan Payne Carter, Paige Marta Skiba, "The Pawn Industry and Its

Customers: The United States and Europe," Law and Economics Working Paper No. 12-26, Vanderbilt University Law School (2012), 5; Heiko Schrader, "The Role of Pawnshops in the Life Strategies of Lower Income Groups: A Preliminary Study in St. Petersburg/Russia," Working Paper No. 316, Universität Bielefeld, Sociology of Development Research Centre.

55 William A. H. Hows, *A History of Pawnbroking: Past and Present* (London: W. Jackson, 1847), 30.

56 For an excellent analysis of this, see Woloson, *In Hock: Pawning in America*, 9-11.

57 Ibid., 17, 21-53.

58 Abdul-Razak, "Economic and Religious Significance," 30.

59 Ibid., 33.

60 Chekhovskich and Schrader, "The History of Pawnshops in Russia," 12-14.

61 Hilary Osborne, "Payday lenders and pawn shops change the face of Britain's high streets," *The Guardian*, May 26, 2012, http://www.theguardian.com/money/2012/may/26/payday-lenders-pawnbrokers-britains-high-streets.

62 John P. Caskey, "Pawnbroking in America: The Economics of a Forgotten Credit Market," *Journal of Money, Credit, and Banking*, 23, 1 (February 1991): 95; Wendy Woloson, "A Brief History of the American Pawn Shop: Echoes," in *Bloomberg News*, February 9, 2012, http://www.bloomberg.com/news/2012-02-09/a-brief-history-of-the-american-pawn-shop-echoes.html.

63 Woloson, "A Brief History of the American Pawnshop."

64 Woloson, *In Hock: Pawning in America*, 16.

65 Larry Allen, *Encyclopedia of Money* (Santa Barbara, CA: ABC-CLIO, 1999), 170.

66 Alan Dundes, *Sacred Narrative, Readings in the Theory of Myth* (Berkeley: University of California Press, 1984), 282.

67 Ibid.

68   Cecilia F. Klein, *"Teocuitlatl,* 'Divine Excrement': The Significance of 'Holy Shit' in Ancient Mexico," *Art Journal,* 52, 3, Scatological Art (Autumn 1993): 25.

69   Charles Perrault, *The Complete Fairy Tales* (Oxford: Oxford University Press, 2009).

70   Ibid.

71   Ibid.

72   Gary Urton, *Inca Myths* (Austin: University of Texas Press, 1999), 69.

73   Michael Taussig, *My Cocaine Museum* (Chicago: University of Chicago Press, 2004), xv.

74   Anne Richter, Bruce W. Carpenter, David A. Henkel, Jörg Sundermann, *Gold Jewellery of the Indonesian Archipelago* (Singapore: Editions Didier Millet, 2012), 154.

75   Renate Sohnen, Peter Schreiner, *Brahmapurāna: Summary of Contents, with Index of Names and Motifs* (Wiesbaden: O. Harrassowitz, 1989), 216.

76   Marc Shell, *Art & Money* (Chicago: University of Chicago Press, 1995), 24.

77   Taussig, *My Cocaine Museum,* 7.

78   "Gold Death-Mask," *National Museum of the Philippines,* http://www.nationalmuseum.gov.ph/nationalmuseumbeta/Collections/Archaeo/Deathmask.html.

79   "Funerary Mask 10th century or earlier," *National Gallery of Australia,* http://www.nga.gov.au/EXHIBITION/LIFEDEA THMAGIC/Default.cfm?IRN=198628&MnuID=3&ViewID =2.

80   "Death in the Americas: Death Mask of the Quimbaya, Colombia," *British Museum,* http://www.britishmuseum .org/explore/young_explorers/discover/museum_explorer/a mericas/death/death_mask.aspx.

81   "Funerary Mask," *The Metropolitan Museum of Art,* http://www.metmuseum.org/collections/search-the-collections/50002534.

82 "The Gold Death Masks of Tutankhamun – The Boy Pharoah," *BBC*, http://www.bbc.co.uk/dna/ptop/A19877845.

83 Notaria Primera de Quibdó, Chocó, Quibdó, Colombia, Libro de venta de esclavos de 1810, ff 134r-v.

84 Ibid., ff 139r.

85 For the global life of Colombian gold, see María Mercedes Botero, *La ruta del oro: una economía primaria exportadora: Antioquia, 1850-1890* (Medellín: Fondon Editorial Universidad EAFIT, 2007).

86 "A la mina no voy" is a famous slave protest song with historical origins in the Cauca region of Colombia during the nineteenth century, and later became part of the grander Andean protest music movement in the 1960s. In Colombia, the Afro-Colombian cumbia vocalist, Leonor Gonzalez Mina, popularized this song in the 1960s. See Cielo Patricia Escobar, *Al ritmo de nuestro folclor* (San Pablo: Editorial San Pablo, 1997), 96.

87 "Hostages in Our Own Territories: Afro-Colombian Rights under Siege in Chocó," Washington Office on Latin America, April 27, 2012, http://www.wola.org/comment ary/hostages_in_our_own_territories.

88 Henry Kamen, *Empire: How Spain Became a World Power, 1492-1763* (New York: Harper Collins, 2003), 42.

89 J. H. Elliott, *Empires of the Atlantic World: Britain and Spain in America, 1492-1830* (New Haven: Yale University Press, 2006), 99.

90 Peter L. Bernstein, *The Power of Gold: The History of an Obsession* (New York: Wiley, 2000), 20.

91 Kamen, *Empire*, 239.

92 Patience Essah, "The Gold Coast," in *The Historical Encyclopedia of World Slavery*, ed. Junius P. Rodriguez (Santa Barbara, California: ABC-CLIO, 1997), 307.

93 Bernstein, *The Power of Gold*, 116. In the early 1700s, the Gold Coast would transform into the Slave Coast, as gold

lost its lure, demand for sugar in the New World grew, and African slaves became the principal commodity to be traded across the Atlantic.

94 James Lockhart, Stuart Schwartz, *Early Latin America: A History of Colonial Spanish America and Brazil* (Cambridge: Cambridge University Press, 1983), 73.

95 Ibid., 64.

96 Kamen, *Empire*, 117

97 Ibid., 108-109.

98 Orián Jiménez, *El Chocó, un paraíso del demonio: Nóvita, Citará y el Baudó, siglo XVIII* (Medellín, Colombia: Editorial Universidad de Antioquia: Universidad Nacional de Colombia, Sede Medellín, 2004), 1.

99 William Sharp, *Slavery on the Spanish Frontier: The Colombian Chocó, 1680-1810* (Norman: University of Oklahoma Press, 1976), 21.

100 Ibid., 112-136.

101 Jiménez, *El Chocó, un paraíso del demonio*, 25.

102 Kathleen J. Higgins, *"Licentious Liberty" in a Brazilian Gold-Mining Region: Slavery, Gender, and Social Control in Eighteenth-century Sabará, Minas Gerais* (University Park, Pa.: Pennsylvania State University Press, 1999), 1-13.

103 Bernstein, *The Power of Gold*, 8.

104 Gavin Jones, "Analysis: Pawn shops proliferate as Italians sell off gold to survive," *Reuters*, August 21, 2012, http://www.iol.co.za/business/business-news/analysis-pawn-shops-proliferate-as-italians-sell-off-gold-to-survive-1.1366533#.UM3wSo6W7qF.

105 "Ghana Gold," Africa Investigates, *Al Jazeera*, November 30, 2011, http://www.aljazeera.com/programmes/africainvestigates/2011/11/2011113071310331931.html.

106 Ibid.

107 "Workers killed in Ghana gold mine collapse," *Al Jazeera*, April 16, 2013, http://www.aljazeera.com/news/africa/2013

/04/201341610298742116.html.

108 "More than 60 killed in gold mine collapse in Sudan's Darfur," *Reuters*, May 2, 2013, http://www.reuters.com/ article/2013/05/02/us-sudan-mine-idUSBRE9410N I20130502.

109 Heather Walsh, "In Colombia, gold mining's becoming more dangerous than cocaine," *Financial Post*, November 10, 2012, http://business.financialpost.com/2011/10/12/gold-mining-becoming-more-dangerous-than-cocaine-to-columbia/.

110 Niki Kitsantonis, "In Greece's Sour Economy, Some Shops Are Thriving," *New York Times*, January 2, 2012, http://www.nytimes.com/2012/01/03/world/europe/as-greece-struggles-pawnbrokers-prosper.html?_r=0.

111 Ioanna Fotiadi, "Pawnshops flourish in crisis," *Ekathimerini*, October 21, 2011, http://www.ekathimerini.com/4dcgi/_ w_articles_wsite4_1_21/10/2011_411370.

112 Daniel Flynn and Renee Maltezou, "Selling gold teeth to make ends meet in Greece," *Reuters*, June 30, 2011, http://www.reuters.com/article/2011/06/30/us-greece-gold-idUSTRE75T5BL20110630.

113 Fotiadi, "Pawnshops flourish in crisis."

114 Kitsantonis, "In Greece's Sour Economy."

115 Ibid.

116 Georgios Karatzas, "Athens: The Image of Modern Hellenism," in *Heritage, Ideology, and Identity in Central and Eastern Europe: Contested Pasts, Contested Presents*, ed. Matthew Rampley (Woodbridge, Suffolk: Boydell Press, 2012), 165.

117 Harry Papachristou and Rosalind Russell, "Hard-Up Greeks Warned: Take Care Selling the Family Jewels," *Reuters*, December 13, 2011, http://www.reuters.com /article/2011/12/14/us-greece-austerity-idUSTRE7B C20J20111214.

118 Fotiadi, "Pawnshops flourish in crisis."

119 Ibid.

120 Renee Maltezou and Peter Graff, "Greek burglars cash in as savers flee banks," *Reuters*, May 24, 2012, http://in. reuters.com/article/2012/05/24/greece-burglars-idINDEE84N0E920120524.

121 Kitsantonis, "In Greece's Sour Economy."

122 Fotiadi, "Pawnshops flourish in crisis."

123 Renee Maltezou and Peter Graff, "Greek burglars."

124 Ibid.

125 Antonis A. Ellinas (2013): "The Rise of Golden Dawn: The New Face of the Far Right in Greece," *South European Society and Politics*, DOI: 10.1080/13608746.2013.782838: 6.

126 For more, see Helena Smith, "Golden Dawn MP's live TV assault shocks Greece," *The Guardian*, June 7, 2012, http://www.guardian.co.uk/world/2012/jun/07/golden-dawn-tv-assault-greece.

127 Nathalie Savaricas, "Anti-fascist fury in Athens after far-right MP hit rival," *The Independent*, June 9, 2012, http://www.independent.co.uk/news/world/europe/antifascist-fury-in-athens-after-farright-mp-hit-rival-7831958.html.

128 Interview with Eliana, April 7, 2013.

129 Ellinas, "The Rise of Golden Dawn," 6.

130 Ibid.

131 Ibid.

132 Ibid., 7.

133 Michael Taussig, *Law in a Lawless Land: Diary of a Limpieza in Colombia* (Chicago: University of Chicago Press, 2005), xiii.

134 Ellinas, "The Rise of Golden Dawn," 8.

135 Human Rights Watch, "Hates on the Streets: Xenophobic Violence in Greece," July 2012: 4. To access their report, see http://www.hrw.org/features/greece-hate-on-the-streets.

136 Sappho Xenakis, "A New Dawn? Change and Continuity in Political Violence in Greece," in *Terrorism and Political*

Violence, Vol. 24, Issue 3 (2012): 445.

137 Human Rights Watch, "Hates on the Streets: Xenophobic Violence in Greece," 25.

138 Ibid., 24.

139 Ibid., 18.

140 Ibid., 13.

141 Liz Alderman, "As Golden Dawn Rises in Greece, Anti-Immigrant Violence Follows," *New York Times*, July 10, 2012, http://www.nytimes.com/2012/07/11/world/europe/as-golden-dawn-rises-in-greece-anti-immigrant-violence-follows.html?pagewanted=all.

142 Ellinas, "The Rise of Golden Dawn," 8.

143 Human Rights Watch, "Hates on the Streets: Xenophobic Violence in Greece," 13.

144 For more information on Shehzad's case, see http://www.enet.gr/?i=news.el.ellada&id=336690 (in Greek) and http://blog.occupiedlondon.org/2013/01/18/murderers-of-26-year-old-serdar-yakoub-had-stash-of-golden-dawn-leaflets-in-their-house/.

145 Yannis Behrakis and Renee Maltezou, "Anti-racism protestors rally in Athens after stabbing," *Reuters*, January 19, 2013, http://www.reuters.com/article/2013/01/19/us-greece-protest-idUSBRE90I0DH20130119.

146 Human Rights Watch, "Hates on the Streets: Xenophobic Violence in Greece," 6.

147 Chloe Hadjimatheou, "The tourists held by Greek police as illegal migrants," *BBC News*, January 10, 2013, http://www.bbc.co.uk/news/magazine-20958353.

148 See the travel advisory here: http://travel.state.gov/travel/cis_pa_tw/cis/cis_1127.html (accessed April 9, 2013).

149 Aris Chatzistefanou, "Golden Dawn has infiltrated Greek police, claims officer," *The Guardian*, October 26, 2012, http://www.guardian.co.uk/world/2012/oct/26/golden-dawn-infiltrated-greek-police-claims.

150 Maria Margaronis, "Greek anti-fascist protesters 'tortured by police' after Golden Dawn clash," *The Guardian*, October 9, 2012, http://www.guardian.co.uk/world/2012/oct/0 9/greek-antifascist-protesters-torture-police.

151 Alderman, "As Golden Dawn Rises in Greece."

152 Sandy Rashty, "Neo-Nazis Golden Dawn plan to open nursery schools," *The Jewish Chronicle*, March 15, 2013, http://www.thejc.com/news/world-news/103370/neo-nazis-golden-dawn-plan-open-nursery-schools.

153 "Golden Dawn nationalists hand out 'Greeks only' food," *BBC News*, August 1, 2012, http://www.bbc.co.uk/news/world-europe-19084584.

154 John Carlin, "Return of the far right: Greece's financial crisis has led to a rise in violent attacks on refugees," *The Independent*, March 30, 2013, http://www.independent.co.uk/news/world/europe/return-of-the-far-right-greeces-financial-crisis-has-led-to-a-rise-in-violent-attacks-on-refugees-8551798.html.

155 Helena Smith, "Greek police send crime victims to neo-Nazi 'protectors,'" *The Guardian*, September 28, 2012, http://www.guardian.co.uk/world/2012/sep/28/greek-police-victims-neo-nazi?CMP=twt_gu.

156 Taussig, *Law in a Lawless Land*, 30.

157 Helena Smith, "Greek police send crime victims to neo-Nazi 'protectors.'"

158 Human Rights Watch, "Hates on the Streets: Xenophobic Violence in Greece," 11.

159 Yiannis Baboulias, "An Antifascist Rapper Was Murdered in Athens Last Night," *Vice*, September 18, 2013, http://www.vice.com/read/the-golden-dawn-murdered-an-antifascist-rapper-last-night.

160 Nikous Dimou, *On the Unhappiness of Being Greek* (Winchester, UK: Zero Books, 2013), 17.

161 For more, see http://en.contrainfo.espiv.net/2011/12/01/pet

ralona-athens-direct-action-against-a-pawn-shop/.

162 For more, see http://en.contrainfo.espiv.net/2012/10/16 /igoumenitsa-greece-direct-attack-on-gold-buying-store/.

163 Mark Lowen, "Greece bartering system popular in Volos," *BBC News*, April 11, 2012, http://www.bbc.co.uk/news /world-europe-17680904.

164 Rachel Donadio, "In Greece, Barter Networks Surge," *New York Times*, October 1, 2011, http://www.nytimes.com /2011/10/02/world/europe/in-greece-barter-networks-surge.html?pagewanted=all&_r=0.

165 "Thousands of workers protest disputed mines in Athens," *Press TV*, March 13, 2013, http://www.presstv.ir/detail/ 2013/03/13/293401/thousands-of-workers-protest-disputed-gold-mine-in-athens.

166 Suzanne Daley, "Seeking Revenue, Greece Approves New Mines, But Environmentalists Balk," *New York Times*, January 13, 2013, http://www.nytimes.com/2013/01/14/ world/europe/seeking-revenue-greece-approves-new-mines-but-environmentalists-balk.html?pagewanted =all&_r=0.

167 Dimou, *On the Unhappiness of Being Greek*, 4.

168 "Thousands of workers protest disputed mines in Athens."

169 Daley, "Seeking Revenue, Greece Approves New Mines."

170 "Thousands of workers protest disputed mines in Athens."

171 Daley, "Seeking Revenue, Greece Approves New Mines."

172 Ibid.

173 "Arsonists attack Hellas gold mine in northern Greece," *BBC News*, February 17, 2013, http://www.bbc.co.uk/ news/world-europe-21489779.

174 For more, see http://londonminingnetwork.org/2013/03/ gold-mining-in-halkidiki-greece-local-peoples-voice-will-not-be-silenced/.

175 Daley, "Seeking Revenue, Greece Approves New Mines."

176 Laura Gottesdiener, *A Dream Foreclosed: Black America and*

the Fight for a Place to Call Home (Westfield, N.J.: Zuccotti Park Press, 2013), 70.

177 Ibid., 74.

178 "Ireland Austerity: Hospitals to send some patients home on weekends," NBC News, August 30, 2012, http://worldnews.nbcnews.com/_news/2012/08/31/13586353-ireland-austerity-hospitals-to-send-some-patients-home-on-weekends.

179 "Greece: Doctors strike over plans to close hospital," Euronews, August 23, 2013, http://www.euronews.com/2013/08/23/greece-doctors-strike-over-plans-to-close-hospitals/.

180 Samantha Winslow, "In Chicago and Philadelphia, Closing Schools and Funding Charters," Labornotes, September 20, 2013, http://www.labornotes.org/2013/09/chicago-and-philadelphia-closing-schools-and-funding-charters.

181 David Stuckler and Sanjay Basu, "Europe's Public Health Disaster: How Austerity Kills," CNN, September 9, 2013, http://edition.cnn.com/2013/09/09/business/europes-public-health-disaster-how-austerity-kills/.

182 Andrew Bashi, "Austerity Kills: Greeks Declare 'Financial Murder' at Funeral of Elderly Man," In These Times, April 9, 2012, http://inthesetimes.com/ittlist/entry/13013/austerity_kills_greeks_declare_financial_murder_in_suicide_of_elderly_man/.

183 Keiji Nakazawa, Hiroshima: The Autobiography of Barefoot Gen (Lanham, MD: Rowman & Littlefield Publishers, 2010), 127.

184 Sublime, "Pawn shop."

Contemporary culture has eliminated both the concept of the public and the figure of the intellectual. Former public spaces – both physical and cultural – are now either derelict or colonized by advertising. A cretinous anti-intellectualism presides, cheerled by expensively educated hacks in the pay of multinational corporations who reassure their bored readers that there is no need to rouse themselves from their interpassive stupor. The informal censorship internalized and propagated by the cultural workers of late capitalism generates a banal conformity that the propaganda chiefs of Stalinism could only ever have dreamt of imposing. Zer0 Books knows that another kind of discourse – intellectual without being academic, popular without being populist – is not only possible: it is already flourishing, in the regions beyond the striplit malls of so-called mass media and the neurotically bureaucratic halls of the academy. Zer0 is committed to the idea of publishing as a making public of the intellectual. It is convinced that in the unthinking, blandly consensual culture in which we live, critical and engaged theoretical reflection is more important than ever before.